CONCORDE

Front cover:
Air France Concorde. *Air France*

Back cover, top:
British Airways Concorde. *BA*

Back cover, bottom:
Concorde production at Filton. 206, 208, 210 and 212 are in this assembly hall picture. *BAC*

Concorde G-BOAD 210 after take-off, carrying the new airline titles. *BAe*

MODERN CIVIL AIRCRAFT
CONCORDE
Philip Birtles

G-BOAD

LONDON
IAN ALLAN LTD

Contents

First published 1984

ISBN 0 7110 1433 7

Published by Ian Allan Ltd, Shepperton, Surrey;
and printed by Ian Allan Printing Ltd at their works
at Coombelands in Runnymede, England.

United States distribution by

Publishers & Wholesalers Inc
Osceola, Wisconsin 54020, USA ®

**Air France Concorde F-BVFA 205 made its maiden flight
from Toulouse 25 October 1975 and was the initial
delivery aircraft.** *Air France*

Preface

When I started writing this book in early 1983, the future of Concorde did not look at all promising, with rumours of withdrawal from service by both airlines in 1984. However, by the time the book was completed much had changed. British Airways is now making a profit of approximately £12million per year on a turnover of £76million using a fleet of six Concordes. Overall profits into the next century are expected to exceed the annual £76million turnover. Air France has reduced its deficit to £1million per year and expects to break even in 1984.

British Airways is now researching an expansion of the Concorde routes to increase utilisation from about 1,000hr/year, which is approximately a quarter of the hours flown by an average jumbo jet. It is planned to extend the Washington DC service to Miami, the 1,000-mile flight taking only 90min, and allowing a possible extension to other destinations, such as Mexico City. The Gulf service may recommence after a four-year break, to an as yet undisclosed country on a twice weekly basis.

Plans are being made to refurbish the fleet, including the return to service of the seventh aircraft, which had been partly cannibalised for spares. Cabin service is to be improved with a new outlook towards catering.

Concorde remains as popular as ever, with about 80,000 passengers/year carried by British Airways, despite a reduction in normal first class travel. Operating costs have been reduced significantly and the aircraft has an assured life of 20 years. Concorde is therefore set to continue operating into the next century, when it will almost certainly be replaced by a high capacity, quieter, more economic aircraft.

My thanks in the preparation of this book to Air France, British Airways, Brennards News Agency, Aerospatiale and British Aerospace at Filton for their help in supplying the many illustrations required for this book.

I am extremely grateful to Air France, in particular Francine Machenaud and Bob Harris, Public Relations Department, for truly memorable flights between Paris and New York.

My thanks also to Julia.

Philip Birtles

1 The Aircraft is Conceived

Without doubt, Concorde was one of the biggest steps in the progress of aviation, equivalent in its impact to the first controlled flight by the Wright Brothers, the first jet-powered flight, the breaking of the sound barrier, the de Havilland Comet becoming the world's first commercial jet airliner, and the placing of a man on the moon. Concorde achieved the seemingly technically impossible task of flying the ordinary airline passenger at twice the speed of sound, a performance which had only previously been possible with military aircraft operated by well protected aircrew. Add to these technological problems the political, economic and environmental objections — always vociferous, often ill-informed and over-emotional — and it is amazing that the aircraft survived to enter airline service.

It became a political aeroplane which, with falling travel demands in an industry suffering from an over-capacity, was the last thing the airlines wanted. The cost of operation had rocketed with the unpredicted fuel crisis, and with all its

seats filled to achieve a profit, the airlines would lose money on the wide-bodied jets with the loss of lucrative first class passengers to the faster service.

Concorde development was a very lengthy programme, from initiation to service entry, and many of the problems that arose could not have been predicted far enough in advance, although it was patently obvious that the initial cost estimates produced at Farnborough were purely imaginative, and could not bear any relation to established facts.

Supersonic airliner studies commenced in Britain in 1955 when enough aerodynamic progress had been made on lift/drag ratios to allow a commercially feasible aircraft to be considered. Through the then Ministry of Supply, the government set up the Supersonic Transport Aircraft Committee (STAC) consisting of 24 members, including representatives of the nine current air-

Concorde prototype 001 F-WTSS was demonstrated at the Paris Air Show in June 1971. *Philip Birtles*

frame companies, four engine companies, the two national airlines, and the government Royal Aircraft Establishment (RAE). Chaired by Morien (later Sir Morien) Morgan, this committee's task was to co-ordinate the preliminary research into the feasibility of the Supersonic Transport (SST), and suggest likely configurations to fit the projected aircraft. The initial meeting was held on 1 October 1956.

In the event two categories of SST were suggested, one a medium range aircraft of about 1,500 miles (2,414km) range, cruising at about Mach 1.3, and the other a longer range aircraft, flying about 3,450 miles (5,552km) at a cruising speed of Mach 1.8 to 2.0. The long range aircraft represented what was believed to be the fastest it was possible to travel using conventional aluminium alloys for the major structure. Significantly greater speeds would have created high temperatures in the structure due to kinetic heating, resulting in the use of the more expensive and difficult to fabricate metals such as

The British assembled prototype 002 G-BSST took part in the SBAC display at Farnborough in September 1972. *Philip Birtles*

stainless steel and titanium.

The research programme was shared amongst the facilities at the RAE and the aircraft manufacturers, later being joined by the Air Registration Board, the Aircraft Research Association, the National Physical Laboratory and the College of Aeronautics at Cranfield. A number of aircraft configurations were considered including an M-wing layout for the medium range aircraft, involving a forward swept wing on the inboard section and a swept-back outer section, with the engines mounted at the join. More common layouts were the delta wing with a thick section containing a submerged fuselage — as favoured by Avro — and the more conventional fuselage

The BAC assembled pre-production Concorde 01 G-AXDN flew by at the Farnborough show in September 1974 during its test programme. The nose is drooped in the landing configuration. *Philip Birtles*

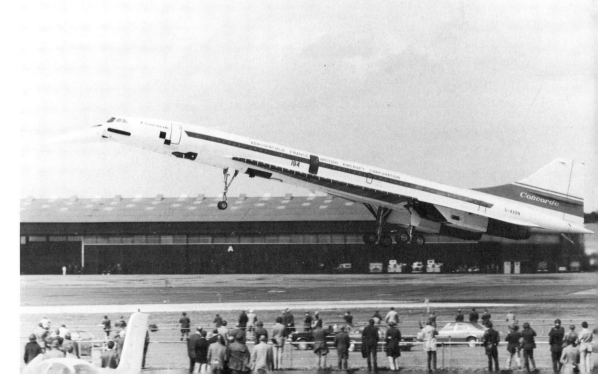

and slender delta wing favoured by Bristol.

The STAC made its formal report to the Ministry of Supply on 9 March 1959, summarising the research work undertaken and recommending that serious detailed design work should commence as soon as possible on two types of supersonic aircraft, a 100-seat medium range type and a 150-seat longer range version. Any delay in commencing work on the longer range transatlantic aircraft would in effect be a decision to opt out of the long-range supersonic transport field, since Britain would never be able to regain a competitive position.

Of the layouts considered, most were developments of existing conventional shapes which would have given plausible, but inefficient designs, and research had indicated that the slender delta offered the best possible combination of low drag, high lift and simplicity. The supersonic aircraft also had to be capable of good low speed performance for approach and landing, retaining stability and controllability throughout the wide performance envelope. To achieve an adequate payload the structure had to be as light as possible, but achieve sufficient strength to resist vibration and flutter. The powerplants would have to be integrated into the overall design to minimise aerodynamic and structural upset of the aircraft, and not be excessively noisy. The aircraft would need to be capable of operating within the current framework of commercial aviation, using the existing ground aids, operational procedures, runways, terminal facilities and complying with safety requirements.

Finally, the aircraft would have to be commercially attractive.

Engine noise would be one of the most intractable problems, although as far as power was concerned, the basis for a suitable engine already existed in the form of the Bristol Olympus. However, it had to form part of an overall propulsive system including a variable geometry air intake, engines optimised for lengthy operation at high temperatures, reheat, jet-pipes and nozzles with some form of noise suppression and reverse thrust for landing.

Supersonic flight was seen to present many new problems in technical, performance, airworthiness, operational and safety aspects requiring a substantial increase in the amount of testing and proving, both on rigs and in the air.

The STAC report predicted a market of between 150 and 500 SSTs, the lower estimate being in line with the Ministry of Transport & Civil Aviation, and the higher one being a Vickers-Armstrong forecast. Too little was known to predict operating costs at such an early stage, but advances in aerodynamic and engine efficiency suggested a parity with existing subsonic aircraft.

The Bristol Aircraft Co concentrated its efforts on a Mach 2 transatlantic aircraft, studying Ogee and Gothic-type slender delta wings in parallel using a unified wing-to-fuselage arrangement. The resulting aircraft featured an Ogee wing,

French built first production Concorde 201 F-WTSB was retained by Aerospatiale at Toulouse for continuing development flying.

The first British built production aircraft 202 G-BBDG appeared in the Farnborough static park in September 1976. *Philip Birtles*

Concorde 202 G-BBDG was retained by BAC for continuing development flying, returning to Filton when Concorde flight operations were moved out of Fairford. *BAC*

giving the best prospects for economic operation and reasonable low speed handling. Power was to come from six Olympus 591 engines, grouped three per side in underwing nacelles.

The feasibility study so clearly pointed the way that in October 1960 the British Aircraft Corporation (BAC) — formed by the merging of the aviation interests of Bristol, English Electric and Vickers — was awarded a design study contract valued at £350,000 to continue work. The resulting submission made in August 1961 was similar to the feasibility study, with an all-up weight of 385,000lb (174,633kg), a payload of 33,000lb (14,970kg) representing 136 passengers, and a range of 3,750 miles (6,035km). Power was from six Bristol Siddeley Olympus 593/3 engines developing 26,700lb (12,110kg) of thrust each. A Mach 3 steel and titanium project was submitted as the same time, but was rejected on the grounds of cost and timescale. Over the North Atlantic route, whereas speeds of Mach 2 could halve the journey time over the subsonic jets, speeds of Mach 3 would save only an additional 10% of the time.

During 1961, doubts about the weight of the aircraft increasing the intensity of the sonic boom, and reservations of the design installation and economics of a six-engine layout, called for a smaller aircraft. Retaining the same overall layout as the six-engined aircraft, the Bristol Type 223 was scaled down to carry about 110 passengers across the North Atlantic at a cruising speed of Mach 2.2. The reduction in size gave a considerable weight saving, allowing a change to four Olympus 593/3 engines. The all-up weight was estimated as 260,000lb (117,935kg) with a payload of 23,000lb (10,432kg).

Even these estimates of weight underline one of the major design problems of an SST. The payload is less than 9% of the total weight. In practice, this became closer to 6% leaving very little margin for error in exceeding weight estimates, loss of power in the engines, or increase in drag. The aircraft could soon end up

The high power of the Rolls-Royce Olympus engines gives Concorde a dramatic climb after take-off. As G-BBDG leaves Fairford the undercarriage is beginning to retract.

with no payload at all, whereas with the current wide-bodied subsonic jet aircraft, the payload tends to be more in the region of 20% of the overall weight, allowing a rather more generous margin for error.

When the design study contract was awarded by the government in 1960, one of the major conditions was that BAC should make every effort to explore the possibilities of international collaboration. The design, development and production of such an aircraft was obviously going to make heavy demands on finance, manpower and facilities. There were definite advantages in sharing with another country if a general agreement could be reached on design principles, not only increasing the potential home market, but also to produce an aircraft with a wider appeal.

Approaches were made by BAC to the United States of America, West Germany and France. The United States of America was already considering an SST, but its proposals were for a larger, longer range Mach 3 aircraft, using more exotic and expensive heat resistant materials, such as stainless steel and titanium. Britain had already built two examples of the high speed Bristol T188 research aircraft, using stainless steel construction. Their protracted construction period had underlined the problems with a comparatively small and simple single-seat short-range experimental aircraft. The Americans were looking at a variety of ways of tackling the problem, including schemes based on the B-70 bomber, swing-wing designs and slender deltas,

but there was little interest or common ground on which to collaborate. The aerospace industry in Germany was still too small and inexperienced to face such a major challenge as a supersonic airliner. More time would be needed to consider such a step.

The French, however, had already been investigating the possibilities of supersonic travel, on very similar lines to Britain. They had a viable aircraft industry with experience in high performance combat aircraft and commercial airliners, but less experience with jet engines. Sud Aviation at Toulouse had produced the Caravelle and, like Bristol Aircraft, was working on an SST, when it too was merged into a larger grouping, becoming part of Aerospatiale. The French had considered both the medium and long range types and, following Caravelle experience, had decided to concentrate on the smaller medium range, less demanding aircraft, allowing growth later in development as experience was acquired.

The earliest recorded meeting between the prospective British and French partners was held at Filton in April 1960, where it was assumed that a similar aircraft would be produced to cover the two requirements, Britain concentrating on the long range transatlantic aircraft and France on the 1,900nm (3,520km) range 60-70 passenger Caravelle replacement. The overall layout would have to be common, with the same fuselage shape and dimensions in the cockpit and cabin. The powerplants and their installation would be similar; initially the heavier long range aircraft having six engines, and the medium range one having four. Much of the equipment, systems and instrumentation could be common to both types.

There were obvious potential advantages in close collaboration between Britain and France on

Below:
With the current financial success of Concorde operations for British Airways, plans are being made to extend the services. *BA*

Bottom:
Air France normally keeps a Concorde at Kennedy Airport, New York to fly to Paris following the arrival of another aircraft in the morning. *Philip Birtles*

supersonic airliners, combining the expertise of the national industries and saving much duplication of effort in research and development. Informal meetings continued between the prospective partners until June 1961, when the first formal meeting was held in Paris. At the Paris Air Show the previous month Sud had shown a model of its proposed SST Super Caravelle, demonstrating the similar lines of development to BAC. Meanwhile Bristol Siddeley, later to become part of Rolls-Royce, had realised that the development of a suitable engine would also have to be a collaborative programme. It had exploratory talks with the

French engine company of SNECMA, and came to a broad agreement that in simple terms Britain would be responsible for the rotating elements, while France would develop the static elements. This agreement, signed on 28 November 1961, paved the way for the choice of this grouping as suppliers of the engine for the proposed SST.

With such a potentially large programme, politics played a major part, probably starting seriously with a meeting in Paris on 7 December 1961 between Peter Thorneycroft, British Minister of Aviation, and Robert Buron, the French Minister of Public Works & Transport. They discussed Anglo-French co-operation on the SST, which was still being considered as two aircraft types covering the medium and long range, though both would be powered by four Bristol-Siddeley Olympus 593 engines, and be similar in many respects to maintain commonality in development. The co-operative programme would be shared financially and technically on a 50/50 basis.

The two design teams had continued in their efforts to bring the proposed aircraft closer together, the leaders having been in regular consultation. The gradual movement towards agreement was a long and sometimes frustrating process, but it built up a trust and confidence which laid the foundation for the collaboration during the years ahead. A sign that agreement was close was at the Farnborough Air Show in September 1962, when a model of the proposed aircraft was shown on the BAC stand. Despite obvious speculation that an Anglo-French agreement to build an SST might be announced, this did not happen for a further two months.

The team leaders most closely concerned with the Concorde project were Dr A. E. (later Sir Archibald) Russell, Technical Director of BAC's Filton Division, and Dr W. J. Strang, the Chief Engineer. In France, Pierre Satre and Lucien Servanty were respectively Technical Director and Chief Engineer of Sud Aviation at Toulouse. In October 1962, a final move was made to complete the protracted negotiations. Bill Strang and Lucien Servanty were shut in a small office in Paris with a draughtsman and drawing board for a day. Their instructions were to produce a three-view general arrangement drawing, to cover a common design for the long range and medium range aircraft. Despite their very contrasting temperaments and personalities, making them an unlikely pair of collaborators for such a demand-

Left:
Concorde cruises at up to 60,000ft, above the disturbance of any weather and clear of other commercial aircraft. *Air France*

Below:
The slim shape of Concorde is improved with the lengthened rear fuselage. G-BOAA 206 first flew from Filton 5 November 1975. *BA*

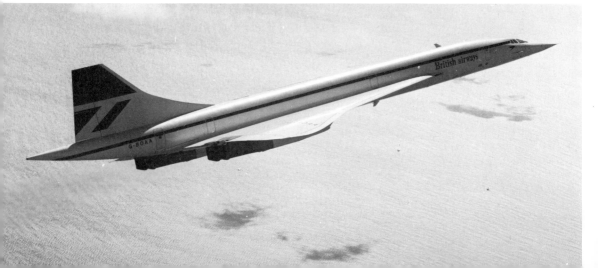

ing programme, they succeeded in evolving a joint proposal, consisting of a slender delta-winged aircraft. The next difficult task was to turn this general understanding into a detailed and definite agreement, allowing design and production to commence.

A joint design study led to detailed technical proposals being made in October 1962 whereby both versions would carry 100 passengers at Mach 2.2, one over stage lengths of up to 2,400nm (4,445km) and the other up to 3,250nm (6,019km). The companies having agreed to work together, and the governments having reached their decision, the historic and binding Anglo-French agreement for the development and production of a civil supersonic transport was signed in London on 29 November 1962. Julian Amery, the current Minister of Aviation, signed for Britain, and Geoffrey de Courcel, the French Ambassador to Britain, signed for France.

With hindsight, this document contained the ingredients for both success and error, but the end result was a technically successful airliner. Perhaps the greatest problem was the unwieldy decision-making process with bi-national boards of directors responsible for airframe and engines, supervised by a standing committee of civil servants from the two countries. Therefore the whole complex programme was to be managed by committee and all decisions taken by overall agreement, with no single final decision maker. Although this had the advantage of producing a better product, it caused unnecessary delay and almost certainly contributed towards the increase of costs. It was agreed that the manufacture of parts, sub-assemblies and major transportable assemblies would be divided exclusively between the two countries, but final assembly and flight testing would be carried out in both countires. A similar agreement was reached for the manufacture of the engines. The provisional cost up to certification of the aircraft, but not including series production, was estimated at £135.2million, over the period from 1962 to 1969.

In the agreement, a detailed division of responsibility and work was listed, covering airframe, aerodynamics, systems, manufacture and engines. Within the 50/50 split, it was realised that Bristol Siddeley with the Olympus engine had a larger share of the powerplant than SNECMA, which was responsible for the rear end beyond the turbine flange, including the reheat, variable nozzle, noise suppression jet pipe and thrust reverser. The balance was assessed as 60/40 in favour of Britain, and on this basis the division of work on the airframe was arranged to be 60/40 in favour of France. The individual company structures would undertake the work packages,

using existing facilities, since there was no need to set up new, duplicated ones. A central programme office was formed to co-ordinate the activities of the participants.

Probably the most significant part of the agreement was what was left out, and that was any form of cancellation clause. In later years when successive British governments were attempting to rid themselves of the expense of the SST, the French used this feature to keep the project alive. Their strength of resolve kept the aircraft going through all adversity and political machinations. Britain had originally seen the SST as a co-operative venture providing an entry ticket to the European Economic Community. However, despite commitment to the project, France denied Britain's membership of the Common Market for a further decade; nevertheless the aircraft could only be cancelled if both sides were in agreement. It was in January 1963, when President de Gaulle made it quite clear that he would not support Britain's entry to the Common Market, that the SST gained its official name of Concorde. It was certainly a most appropriate and suitable name, which had been suggested by the 10-year old son of a BAC official. Britain had approved of the name, but tended to wish to spell it the English way, 'Concord'. The French were not enthusiastic about the name, until the surprise confirming announcement by their president. The arguments as to which way to spell the name went on for some time, but the eventual result was the French version. When de Gaulle failed to support Britain's entry he, at the same time — to keep the door open — suggested an accord of association, making the Concorde the major condition of any future negotiations. He therefore quickly forestalled any British thoughts of cancelling the project at that stage.

Britain soon began to realise that to take best advantage of supersonic travel, the long range aircraft was the best prospect. It was only on sector lengths in excess of 1,500 miles (2,414km) that the time saving of the higher cruising speeds became significant. A shorter range Mach 1.2 aircraft would be technologically demanding to produce and at the same time provide very little benefit to the traveller in reducing the duration of the journey. The Mach 2.2 long range aircraft would be a greater challenge, but more worthwhile. France was not convinced, still preferring its Super Caravelle with a more modest performance.

The turning point in the industrial negotiations was the placing of options by Pan American Airways in the summer of 1963. All the airline interest concentrated on the long range version, with no enthusiasm for the medium range aircraft. The French manufacturer's team finally realised its aircraft was still-born and a joint go-ahead was agreed on the transatlantic aircraft. Work then commenced to reallocate the design and manufacturing tasks for the one aircraft type.

It was generally understood that the French would lead on the design side of the project, and the British would lead the manufacturing effort, but this was never precisely defined. It was soon clear that joint direction would be necessary, and agreement was reached that Sir George Edwards, Chairman of BAC, and General Andre Puget, President of Sud-Aviation, would take all major executive decisions jointly, after prior discussion. The original plan had been for them to alternate as chairman and vice-chairman, but in practice the Aircraft Committee had two chairmen.

Fortunately intervention at chairman level was rare, but at the executive and design engineer level there was a continual daily contact by telephone, telex or data link, and on occasions by the regular business jets which flew out each morning and back in the late afternoon. By flying direct from Filton to Toulouse, an engineer was only out of his office for the working day. On scheduled public transport, a one-day meeting would result in three days out of the office, a situation which was often totally unacceptable.

Not unnaturally, one of the communications snags was the different languages. Sud-Aviation had been selling the Caravelle in the international market, requiring a good level of English for many of its engineering and sales executives. The British had in most cases little more than sixth-form French. The normal procedure was for the two companies to conduct meetings in their own national language without immediate translation, resulting in the British engineers gaining a good working knowledge of French in their professional field.

Despite the ideal opportunity to make Concorde an all metric dimensioned aircraft, each country stuck to its own standards of measurement within its own components and assemblies, with structures dimensioned in both scales only on the interface.

It was at this stage that people began to realise that the early cost estimates were somewhat suspect. General Puget had a very close relationship with General de Gaulle, and knew that when funding was required, the President would arrange it with the French Ministry of Finance. This gave him an enormous advantage over his British colleagues, who did not have such easy access to funding when beginning to translate the design into metal. The first rumblings of discontent began to emanate from the Committee of Public Accounts, the House of Commons watchdog on the Concorde estimates. This committee's outspoken criticism caused difficulties for the government and embarrassment to the Treasury. The estimate of £150million to produce the Concorde prototypes was completely speculative, with the government fully committed to the project. Any authorisation was only a formality, and unlike the French officials, the project financiers in the Treasury were not represented on the committee of officials supervising the progress of the project. Even at this stage there appeared to be little prospect of recovering the development funding, even if some 200 were sold. The lack of provision of a cancella-

The underslung engines give Concorde wing a smooth upper surface. *BAe*

Concorde lands with a high nose-up attitude requiring a droop of the nose to improve visibility. Air France Concorde F-BVFB. *Air France*

tion clause was also deplored, which despite strong arguments in favour from the French, had been resisted by Julian Amery.

The British persuasion of the French to accept the one long range supersonic airliner had resulted in some major redesign to optimise it more satisfactorily for the stages anticipated. This of course had further increased the costs although the government gave assurances that cost control was being exercised. The new improved Concorde was launched at the 1964 International Airline Transport Association (IATA) Technical Committee meeting in Beirut. The new Concorde was a larger aircraft capable of carrying up to 118 passengers over ranges of nearly 4,000 miles (6,437km). First flight was planned in 1967, with service entry by 1971.

In the House of Commons on 9 July 1964 Julian Amery was questioned on Concorde costs following his return from a meeting in Paris with the French Minister of Transport. It was almost casually revealed that Britain's half share of the costs was something like £140million, an almost doubling of the previous estimates.

On 16 October 1964 the British Conservative government was replaced by the Harold Wilson-led Labour government with a slender majority. This was committed to getting Britain moving with a series of major decisions in the first 'one hundred days' of government. Despite the planned energetic technological policy giving work to its supporters, the aerospace industry was no favourite of the Wilson administration, whose suspicion was fuelled by an aviation report

compiled by Richard Worcester, an independent aviation consultant and outspoken critic of British aviation. Worcester believed that the bigger and better American SST would outstrip Concorde and that all British military projects should be dropped, and replaced by American aircraft. Moreover, with an £800million deficit in overseas payments in 1964 and a similar prospect for 1965, a serious run on the pound and a number of inflationary projects, the Bank of England urged immediate cuts in government spending. Concorde was an expensive luxury to be axed without delay, together with the more vulnerable BAC TSR2 strike bomber, the Hawker Siddeley HS681 short take-off jet tactical transport and the supersonic P1154 Harrier replacement. In return, Britain could put its skilled work force on the dole, and purchase American transport and combat aircraft. The TSR2 replacement was to be the American F-111, which was ordered, then cancelled to be replaced by an Anglo-French combat aircraft, which was in turn cancelled eventually to be replaced by the British/German/Italian Tornado. The money wasted on the cancelled projects would have certainly seen the TSR2 into service. Lockheed Hercules were purchased from America to cover the RAF transport requirement and Rolls-Royce Spey-engined Phantoms were ordered for interception duties, providing the engine manufacturer with some production work on an aircraft which performs better with its original American engines.

However, Concorde survived, despite American insistence that as a condition of them providing economic assistance to Britain, it should be axed. America could hardly agree to US dollars financing a project which was so competitive to the American aerospace industry. De Gaulle had still to be approached and persuaded to abandon his plan to end American domination of the skies. BAC was advised of the impending cancellation on Saturday, 24 October 1964, by the not unusual method of pointed questions by a reputable journalist. The TSR2 was expected to be cancelled, but the same for Concorde had not been anticipated, as this would mean the closure of the large Filton factory with the loss of thousands of jobs. Sir Pierson Dixon, the British Ambassador in Paris, received his instructions from the British government on Sunday 25 October, to call upon the French Foreign Minister, M. Couve de Murville, and to inform him that Britain wished to cancel Concorde. The French did not understand the British position and sensed some American collusion in the cancellation plans. De Gaulle was enraged by Britain's apparent treachery, and made it quite clear that France had every intention of holding Britain to the agreement signed in November 1962. The French decided to sit tight and let the Wilson government sweat out the problem. The indignation of the prospective loss of technological advance called for a public enquiry. If the money saved by cancellation was to be used for non-productive social programmes, the growth prospects of the economy would suffer.

The French began to investigate co-operation with other countries, should Britain pull out of Concorde, including talks with the Russians on the supply of an alternative engine. It was later found that the major weakness of the Russian SST was its powerplants, but at the time these contacts were carefully leaked to the press by the French. It was also obvious that should Concorde be scrapped, the diplomatic consequences would be considerable. Following a meeting on 19 November the French government delivered its ultimatum to London, stating three clear points: the treaty did not allow for any revision, any delay would help American competition, and Concorde must be built as planned. De Gaulle issued instructions that there should be no further technical contact with BAC until the British government came to its senses.

Harold Wilson had little choice. If Britain unilaterally denounced the treaty, it would have been sued by France in the International Court. Britain would almost certainly have lost, allowing the French to go ahead with the project alone, charging Britain half of whatever the ultimate cost might be, without any benefit from the research or the ultimate aircraft. Britain could therefore not gain any saving in money, but would lose all the technological and any economic advantage, as well as suffering serious diplomatic repercussions.

The French refused any further Concorde discussions, including various alternative slowing

Below:
British Airways Concorde G-BOAB 208 lifting off with the nose and visor drooped for take-off. *BAe*

Right:
Concorde G-BOAE 212, the 12th production aircraft and fifth for British Airways was delivered 20 July 1977. *BAe*

Below right:
British Airways Concorde 214 was originally registered G-BFKW, but later re-registered G-BOAG. *BAe*

down proposals, which only served to increase costs. The only condition of reopening talks was a guarantee from Britain that the treaty would be honoured, while work in the factories was coming to a halt, each delay giving the Americans a chance of catching up on the European four-year lead.

The project was finally saved, from the unexpected direction of the unions involved, whose members were rapidly running out of work, and concerned not unnaturally for their future careers. There was no dramatic change, but gradually the Labour government gained an uneasy acceptance of Concorde. The technological arguments and massive redundancies were major considerations. The turning point was a formal dinner at Chequers on 15 January 1965 when Harold Wilson and his ministers met the aviation industrialists to clarify the position. Soon after this work began to pick up again and the industrialists on either side of the Channel were able to renew their contacts. At least the national teams were more united, having fought together for the project, which helped relations enormously.

Although Concorde had many more hurdles to jump, the worst political one had passed and the remainder of the problems tended to be technical ones with their attendant spiralling costs. The sonic boom was to be another intractable problem which defied solution by financial or technical means, relegating the aircraft to supersonic flights over the oceans or land areas of low population. When flying over populated areas, the speed would have to be reduced to subsonic, making Concorde highly uncompetitive to existing airliners with their more spacious, cheaper first class cabins. Foreign countries had to be persuaded to accept Concorde, and in many cases could turn it down without any constructive reason. The sonic boom, engine noise, and damage to the environment were all easily raised objections, which were difficult, if not impossible, to counter by the manufacturers.

Left:
G-BFKX 216 was the last production Concorde, which first flew from Filton 20 April 1979, and was delivered to British Airways 13 June 1980, later re-registered G-BOAF. The last two aircraft delivered were not originally part of the British Airways order. *BAe*

Below:
Concorde is the flagship of the Air France fleet.
Air France

2 Design and Development

With the agreement to design and develop the Concorde, an exhaustive programme of research had to be undertaken before such a radical aircraft could be certificated for passenger operations. In those early days the overall magnitude and complexity could not have been foreseen. It involved flying specially built or modified research aircraft to determine handling at high and low speeds, and considerable flight testing of the Olympus engine in a Vulcan test bed. This was all in addition to the massive efforts in ground testing. The engineering team was working at the frontiers of technology, and exploring areas not previously experienced. The outcome of much of the research could not be predicted, resulting in more than a decade of work before the maiden flight, and some 5,000 hours of flight development, making it the most thorough and comprehensive civil aircraft programme ever undertaken.

The initial effort had to concentrate principally on the complex aerodynamics, structures and materials, to formulate a basic aircraft design. This allowed preliminary discussions with potential customers to be started, to establish the most commercially attractive aircraft. The installation of the powerplants had a critical effect upon the overall aerodynamics, which was far more demanding than on subsonic aircraft. Not only

had the engines to produce the correct power for each flight condition, but the combination of the wings, air intakes, engines and nozzles had to work smoothly together at all times. These conditions ranged from the extremes of standing still ready for take-off, to flying in excess of Mach 2 at 60,000ft (18,288m) and included smooth transonic acceleration as well as any number of abnormal situations which might arise in an emergency.

Control of the aircraft throughout its flight envelope was also a major challenge. Flaps for take-off and landing could not be used on a tailless slim delta. However, a characteristic of the slender slim delta, not found with other wing shapes, was that sufficient lift could be generated through a wide speed range simply by varying the angle of attack to the airflow. At high speed the angle of attack was small, but at low speeds it increased well above that which would normally cause conventional wings to stall. This feature, called vortex lift, is a result of large, slow-moving swirls of air

The Handley Page HP115 was designed to test the slender delta wing for Concorde at low speed. It first flew from RAE Bedford on 17 August 1961 and is now preserved with the British Concorde prototype 001 as part of the Science Museum display at Yeovilton.
Philip Birtles

enveloping the whole upper surface of the wing, increasing the suction and therefore the lift. Vortex lift is fundamental to Concorde's ability to fly slowly, allowing it to operate into existing airports and traffic patterns.

Conventional trim tab spoilers and similar moving surfaces could not be used in a supersonic airliner, as they caused unacceptable drag at high speeds. The traditional trailing edge control surface movement had to be kept as small as possible for the same reason. It was therefore necessary to use the natural wing structural flexibility, combined with camber and twist shape, to allow the aerodynamic loading to trim itself.

Wing aerodynamics has advanced greatly over the period of the mid-1970s to early 1980s, and now approaches a science. In the design stages of Concorde, it was still very much more of an art. The wing had to be built to a certain estimated shape and flexibility in the jig, to achieve the correct profile in the full range of the flight envelope. It was found to be incorrect in practice on the prototypes where 2° of unwanted deflection resulted in a payload cut of 1,600lb (726kg). To a casual observer, the slim delta wing shape of the Concorde looks beautifully simple, but at close quarters it can be seen to be a most complex aerodynamic form, with an exactly calculated degree of camber and taper across the wing and a precise combination of droop and twist along the leading edge. Even to achieve the relatively unrefined prototype stage required, some 5,000 hours of studies were made in wind tunnels covering the entire speed range and involving the support of a range of high capacity computers. Wind tunnel research always suffers from scale effect, and therefore full scale results cannot be predicted with absolute accuracy.

Amongst the many innovative features of the Concorde was the hinged nose and visor to allow the crew better visibility at the lower speeds when the nose was naturally higher. The configuration changed somewhat from the prototype to the production aircraft, where on the latter the view with the nose up was much improved. For take-off and subsonic cruise, the nose is lowered 5° and the visor is down. As the speed increased after take-off, the nose is raised with the visor remaining retracted. For supersonic flight, the nose and glazed visor are raised. On the approach, landing and movements around the airfield, the nose is drooped to its lowest point of $12\frac{1}{2}°$ with the visor retracted. The original design used on the prototypes had the cockpit windows covered by a mostly metal visor as a protection against kinetic heating, but the development of suitable heat resistant windscreen materials came in time to be incorporated into the production aircraft.

A major change in the fuselage from the prototypes to the production stage was the extension and reshaping of the extreme rear section. The upper line of the fuselage was extended almost horizontally, with the lower line sweeping up to meet it at the tip. Supersonic drag was significantly reduced and it provided the bonus of extra fuel capacity.

Although the fixing of the top speed in the region of Mach 2 allowed the use of aluminium

Concorde droop nose and visor. *BAe*

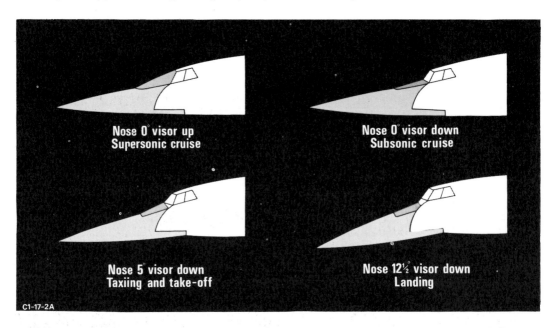

Nose 0° visor up
Supersonic cruise

Nose 0° visor down
Subsonic cruise

Nose 5° visor down
Taxiing and take-off

Nose 12½° visor down
Landing

C1-17-2A

alloy for the structure, there were wide ranges of alloys with both desirable and undesirable properties. One of the problems was due to a phenomenon called creep, which is directly related to supersonic operations. It is the term defining the deformation of metal caused by the interaction of high temperatures and mechanical loadings. Engine designers were already familiar with creep due to the high temperature operation of their products, but it was new to the airframe designer, and especially difficult in the larger scales involved. After exhaustive testing, a copper-based aluminium alloy, known as RR58 in Britain and AU2GN in France, was selected. It had been originally developed for use in gas turbine blades, but now it was required in greater bulk including sheet, billet or forging to whatever raw material size was needed for Concorde. This was

BAC221 prototype was a conversion of one of the two Fairey Delta FD2 research aircraft, for high speed scale testing of Concorde's wing. It first flew in this form from Filton 1 May 1964, and featured a droop nose. *BAe*

only one of the many materials which had to be tested for application in a supersonic airliner, including the various metals, transparencies for the cockpit and cabin and a variety of plastics including the radome, paints, sealants, adhesives and non-ferrous materials.

Another temperature problem was the very basic one of expansion and contraction caused by the kinetic heating and air cooling of the airframe at various speeds. The maximum skin temperatures varied from 127°C at the extreme

A model of Concorde in the high speed wind tunnel. *BAC*

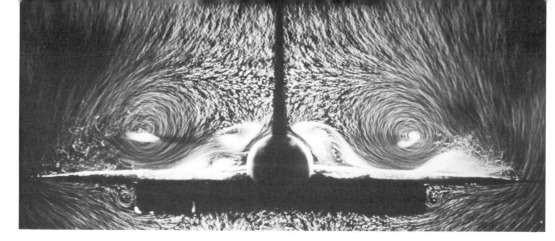

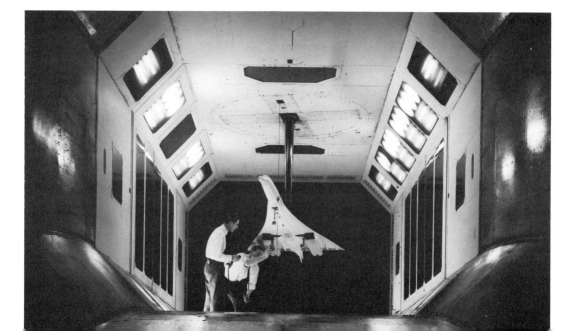

nose to 91°C on the rear cabin. The temperature gradient of the wing varied from 105°C on the leading edge to 91°C at the trailing edge where it joined the fuselage. The expansion variation, not only of different materials but also of the same material at different temperatures, had to be allowed for, to avoid unacceptable stress in the aircraft.

As with all aircraft, Concorde was subjected to a demanding and comprehensive programme of structural testing, commencing with small test pieces, and culminating in full scale testing of two complete specimen airframes. To be effective the laboratory tests had to reproduce the full flight conditions, including the thermal profile of each typical supersonic flight. This ground testing also had to be well ahead of any actual flight hours, to allow a satisfactory safety margin should any weakness be found. To accommodate the Concorde test airframes, two vast new testing facilities had to be built, one for the static load testing at Toulouse in France, and the other for fatigue testing at the Royal Aircraft Establishment (RAE) at Farnborough in England.

At the RAE the fatigue test specimen was covered almost entirely by an outer ducting through which hot and cold air was pumped to reproduce the flight temperature cycle. Hot water was used for heating the air and refrigerated liquid ammonia for cooling. While these temperature variations were being applied some 100 servo-controlled hydraulic jacks were used to apply external loading to the specimen. Internal loads representing cabin pressurisation, air conditioning and fuel movement were also imposed. Concorde presented its own particular problems for pressurisation because of its size. However, the relatively simple answer was to pack the cabin with polystyrene and pressurise the relatively small volume remaining, localising any damage. Subsonic aircraft, without the problems of high temperature, can be pressure tested in water tanks, with the specimen filled with water which is pressurised. If there is a failure of the cabin, the damage is localised because of the low compressibility of water. If the specimen is filled with pressurised air, and there is a failure, it could result in a catastrophic explosion, destroying the

evidence of the failure, together with the specimen and its test facilities.

To speed up the fatigue testing, internal heating and cooling was also provided, taking the temperatures to 120°C, some 20°C more than normally encountered overall in flight. It had been established that this increased temperature for a shorter time had the same effect as a longer heat soak at lower temperatures. The effects of a one-hour cycle on the RAE rig is therefore equivalent to a typical three-hour flight.

The fatigue testing started in August 1973, and by the end of 1974 the certification requirement of 6,800 flight cycles had been achieved successfully. This testing has continued to complete 7,000 flight cycles annually, which results in the test specimen being at least three times more advanced than the earliest aircraft to enter commercial service. In recent years testing has been reduced slightly, due to the aircraft utilisation being lower than predicted, and the airlines are finding the support of these activities a costly exercise.

Static testing of the airframe began much earlier at Toulouse in September 1969, initially at room temperature. The imposition of progressive design loads was then repeated in transient and steady temperature conditions representing in-flight conditions. Kinetic heating was simulated using 35,000 infra-red lamps, and 70,000litres of liquid nitrogen was used for cooling, giving a skin temperature range of +120°C to −10°C within 15 minutes. Meanwhile, 80 servo-controlled hydraulic jacks imposed the structural loading and the test instrumentation was capable of recording and processing 8,000 data points every two seconds.

This test programme was successfully completed in 1972 clearing the airframe to a 385,000lb (174,636kg) take-off weight. Static testing then continued to clear the structure to a take-off weight of 400,000lb (181,440kg) and damage was introduced into critical areas to establish the resistance to fatigue cracks and other failures.

The fatigue testing, which is dynamic, is an essential process to establish the ability of the design to withstand the regularly repeated flight cycle loadings imposed in the course of normal airline operations. The fatigue life of the airframe has to be established to determine the overall safe life of the aircraft, or the points at which some areas or load bearing parts have to be repaired or replaced. Should a fatigue crack appear, the surrounding structure should be capable of withstanding the additional loads without further failure, and the damage should be easily located during routine inspections. The static testing proved the integrity of the airframe

Left, top to bottom:

Concorde relies on vortex lift to allow it to fly at low speeds on approach and landing. This effect can be demonstrated in the wind tunnel. BAe

Many hours of wind tunnel testing were undertaken (some upside down!) on a variety of Concorde models to assess lift, drag and other aerodynamic features. BAe

A low speed wind tunnel model of Concorde is adjusted ready for the next series of tests. BAC

structure and its efficiacy of standing up to the many transient aerodynamic and mechanical loads experienced in flight conditions.

Many other tests had to be made on critical parts of the Concorde structure such as the windscreens, tail-surfaces and undercarriage. The cockpit windscreens were static-tested to failure and the fatigue testing under realistic temperature conditions included introducing deliberate failure in one element, while the remainder were under load. Bird impact tests were conducted to confirm the resistance to impact at low level, and hail impact tests were made. The fin, rudder and rear fuselage were acoustically tested to establish their resistance to high levels of jet noise.

Like the Concorde structure, the systems also had to be capable of operation over a wider range of temperatures than experienced with subsonic operations. Specialised and impressive test rigs had to be constructed to duplicate systems working in the operational environment. Amongst the major test rigs constructed were ones to test hydraulics, electrics, flying controls, fuel management, undercarriage operation and air conditioning. These rigs helped to highlight any design problems on the ground, before the prototypes flew, saving costly flight time on unnecessary tasks.

Aerospatiale's hydraulic rig at Toulouse was a complete full scale replica of the flight control system with its associated hydraulic and electrical

The Concorde wing leading edge is a complicated shape, not a straightforward slim delta. Air France Concorde F-BVFA at Kennedy Airport, USA. *Philip Birtles*

systems, including the undercarriage functioning system. Close by, and capable of interconnection, was the advanced Concorde design flight simulator. Although the simulator was primarily a design tool, it could be used to some extent for basic crew training. The computer-operated rig was used to investigate flight characteristics and control system response before flight testing commenced. It was also linked to the Air Traffic Control at Orly, Paris to study the techniques of integrating Concorde into existing airport operations. The rig continues in use to determine the overall integrity of the systems and the failure rate of any mechanical components, since aerodynamic loads have no effect on the wear and tear of the systems' operation. A particularly valuable part of the testing is the auto-pilot operation, where a continual programme of automatic landings can be simulated, without the expense of flying the aircraft, to achieve the very low failure rate demanded of the components of this system.

Critical to Concorde's operation was a complicated fuel management system. A massive fuel systems test rig was built in full scale at Filton, consisting of a movable platform carrying a complete reproduction of the aircraft's fuel system. While under test, the rig is moved to simulate the normal attitudes and accelerations experienced in

flight, including the actual fuel temperatures and pressures, and rates of climb and descent.

Two full scale rigs were constructed to test the electrical systems, one for the generation and the other for distribution.

The design was 'frozen' early in 1965 at a maximum take-off weight of 326,000lb (147,874kg) with a passenger capacity of 118; this allowed the first metal to be cut for the prototype aircraft. With total options from major airlines for up to 43 aircraft, market prospects for Concorde began to look encouraging. The massive production effort could now commence, with planning of the manufacture and assembly, training of the work force, ordering new machines and construction of the jigs and tools. This was also the stage at which the production engineers from each country began to communicate and learn to work with each other.

Early manufacturing experience was gained in the new materials by building test specimens, initially small assemblies, but eventually the full-sized major units. One of the techniques developed in the production of Concorde was sculpture milling, which is the process of machining large components from solid billets, using computer tape-controlled machine tools. The original billets were either rolled or forged to give some grain flow, and the required shape was carved out of the solid metal. For many years large wing skins had been produced by this means using simple metal templates, but with the

Concorde prototype 001 F-WTSS at Toulouse. It featured the original visor, short fuselage and small tail fairing. *Aerospatiale*

complicated double curvature and multi-taper shapes more sophisticated computer control was required.

This method of manufacture has three major advantages. It provides high structural integrity, weight saving and avoids lengthy assembly work and the associated complex tooling. Any assembled structure, whether it is bolted, riveted or welded, has a source of weakness at the joint. Many of the Concorde components were highly stressed making sculpture milling an ideal answer. Secondly, weight saving can be made due to the tighter tolerances capable with a machining process. Even savings overall of a few hundred pounds are significant with Concorde's low payload capacity. Every unnecessary pound of weight on Concorde requires an additional pound of fuel to fly it across the Atlantic, and that extra pound of fuel requires a further pound of fuel to carry it. Therefore, every pound of weight saved on the structure means three more pounds of payload, making a few hundred pounds in weight saving very significant to the aircraft economics. If a component such as a fuselage frame or wing spar is fabricated from a whole range of parts, none of which is the same, all these parts have to be designed, tooled, manufactured and stored. When the time comes for assembly, they all have to be collected together, placed in a com-

plicated jig, located, drilled, deburred and assembled. An expensive and time consuming process, when the overall need is speed of production at the lowest possible price, to offer the most economic package to an airline.

As with the manufacture of any new product, there is what is known as the learning curve, where the early examples take longer and cost more to build than the later ones when there is a greater familiarity with the work. Concorde suffered particularly badly from the effects represented by the learning curve, as not only was

The two Concorde prototypes featured the original visor with poor visibility when raised. F-WTSS at Toulouse. *BAC*

it a complex aircraft with many innovative features, but in the end its production run was short, not allowing full advantage of the learning to be taken, and it was assembled in two places.

The double assembly line was purely a political requirement, as to assemble and flight test the aircraft in only one country would have been totally unacceptable to the other. A means had to be found to avoid the duplication of effort as much as possible, and therefore the effects of the learning curve making the programme even more expensive. Allowing for the agreed 60/40 split of airframe work in France's favour, the airframe was divided up into manageable sections where there would be no duplication of effort. Broadly, BAC was responsible for the entire nose section including forward cabin (ahead of the wing), the tail-cone, fin and rudder, and the air intake and engine bay. Aerospatiale was responsible for the

Concorde manufacturing break-down. *Bob Downey*

Systems responsibilities:

BAC	AEROSPATIALE
Electrics	Hydraulics
Oxygen	Flying controls
Fuel	Navigation
Engine instrumentation	Radio
Engine controls	Air conditioning supply
Fire	
Air conditioning distribution	
De-icing	

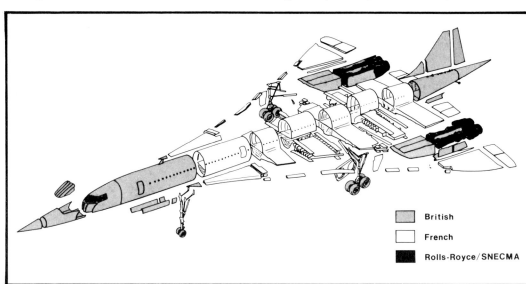

British

French

Rolls-Royce/SNECMA

remainder of the fuselage and the wing with its control surfaces. The sub-assemblies were manufactured and fully equipped in a number of factories in each country and then delivered initially by road and sea, and later by air to the respective production lines. The final assembly was therefore a relatively simple matter of joining the parts and connecting up the systems, involving low manpower. This method has been developed for the European Airbus which only requires some 200 people to assemble four or five aircraft every month. However, in the early stages there are always late deliveries of equipment, due to development and production problems and they have to be installed during final assembly, involving special working parties who are in the way of regular workers on the line.

Production was based initially on a total market for 150 Concordes with a peak build rate of three per month. The two countries adopted completely different assembly techniques, the French going for quantity production tooling from the start, where the aircraft would move through various jigs and stages until it was complete. At Filton, the flexible concept was adopted, where each aircraft was assembled totally in one jig, leaving the options open if, as happened, the programme did not lead to anything substantial. The aim was to achieve identical production methods, but this never happened within the nationally constructed sub-assemblies. However, on the joints there had to be a standardisation. The British technique of joining the fuselage sections was to slide one over the other to obtain a tight fit, but the French had never done it this way and did not believe it was possible. Test pieces were made up to prove the concept, which was being used on many British aircraft currently flying, and now the technique has also been adopted on the Airbus range. These examples do not mean that Britain was always correct, as it had a great deal to learn from the French, but it did result in excellent experience from both industries coming together to achieve the best possible answer.

One example of the problems experienced was with the original French-designed powerplant nozzles. The payload was down to 12,200lb (5,534kg) with both the design and the production of the nozzles causing great difficulty. BAC felt that it could recover around 5,000lb (2,268kg) of payload by redesign, but this was not its responsibility. However, George Edwards encouraged his engineers to solve the problem; they collaborated with a Californian company and came up with a design using a stainless steel honeycomb sandwich structure. This was the one eventually adopted.

Another way that Concorde differs from conventional subsonic jet airliners is that all the available space is packed with the equipment and systems. Today's wide-body jet airliners have large open spaces above the cabin ceiling, but the inside of Concorde is more like the modern military aircraft, making assembly and maintenance more difficult. As with the airframe and powerplants, the systems and equipment supply had to be divided according to the national share, which again led to an inefficient and uneconomic result. All equipment for any aircraft should be commercially and competitively procured to obtain the best price for the most effective

Geographical location of manufacture. *Bob Downey*

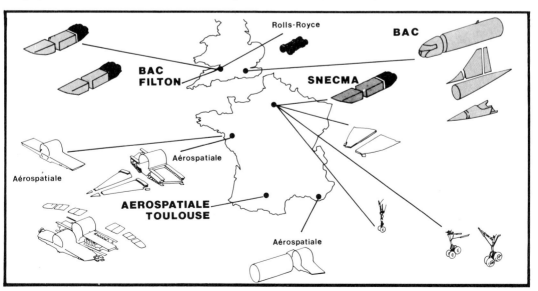

product. Although none of the equipment in Concorde is by any means sub-standard, in a number of cases it is not the ideal answer to the individual specification.

All the equipment was new and required development. For a medium-sized equipment company, a successful bid for a contract was of greater value than the work involved. If one supplier was to find difficulties in the development, there was always someone in the other country ready to take over with something they had been developing as a speculation. The two most outstanding examples were the hydraulic pumps and the generating equipment, where many changes were made. There was a preference for American equipment by both airframe companies, but the governments insisted on buying either British or French. This may seem a very laudable decision, but when trying to sell aircraft in a world market it is no bad thing to have equipment from other nations, particularly America, used in the airliner. This helps politically, industrially and with credibility and maintenance.

Five different generator designs were considered — initially in Britain, because the British were responsible for the power controls; then France; then an Anglo-American design which was fitted to the development aircraft; followed by a return to a UK design. The final change was made to an American design manufactured in Britain to save about 400lb (181kg) weight per aircraft.

Even when the two industrial teams were finally in agreement about a design or production method, their decision could be changed by the government committees. Not only did this result in delay, but was often a wrong choice which later had to be changed, meaning double development.

At the start of the programme the British equipment industry tended to be ahead of the

French, although by the end the two were practically equal. The British companies, through their trade organisations, the Society of British Aerospace Companies (SBAC) and the Electronic Engineering Association (EEA), held regular meetings to lobby the British government to adopt their products. There was a strong belief, that the less advanced French industry was keen to adopt advanced American equipment, which could be licence-built in France, learning the trade of advanced aviation at the expense of British industry and the taxpayer. The British officials were strenuously opposed to the adoption of American equipment unless technically unavoidable, and only then if a British or French company was associated with the development to gain the maximum technological benefit.

The air conditioning system, sub-contracted to Hawker Siddely Dynamics, was a difficult area. In subsonic flight the cabin air had to be warmed, while in supersonic cruise it had to be cooled. The overall responsibility was unfortunately split between the two countries, the French being in charge of the air supply, while Britain was concerned with its distribution. Hawker Siddeley Dynamics was obliged to use a number of components designed and manufactured in France, which did not assist in overall fault finding.

However, it was not all problems to be overcome. A notable British success on the equipment side was the development by Dunlop of the carbon wheel brakes for production Concordes. The French favoured an American design of brakes but in comparative tests the UK design proved superior. As a result of this selection, and the change from the steel brakes on the development aircraft, a weight saving of 1,200lb (544kg) per aircraft was made. The Concorde was the first civil aircraft to be fitted with carbon brakes, and on a number of occasions the aircraft has been saved from further damage during emergency stops on take-off when using this computer-controlled system. Carbon brakes are now also being adopted for a number of new airliners throughout the world, because they are not only lighter but also dissipitate heat more rapidly. This is just one of the many examples of the technological spin-off, from Concorde.

The industrialists felt that it would have been better to have delayed construction of the prototypes until they could have been produced nearer to the pre-production standard, and then launch straight into production. This was, however, politically unacceptable because the aircraft had to be flown as soon as possible to prove the overall concept, even if it was not entirely representative and more costly. Despite all the industrial, political, technical and economic problems, the Concorde was being built and approaching its maiden flight. The critics continued to batter it with journalistic invective, but there was no doubt that it had caught the imagination of many people, and they were enthusiastic to see it fly thereby proving its capabilities in its natural environment. That day was slowly approaching.

Pre-production Concorde 01 G-AXDN and production standard aircraft 202 G-BBDG in the hangar at Filton showing different rear fuselage shapes. *BAe*

Above:
The static test airframe at Toulouse. *BAe*

Left:
The full scale fuel test rig at Filton. *BAe*

Below left:
Concorde assembly at Aerospatiale, Toulouse. Pre-production aircraft 02 is practically complete with 201 beyond and the early stages of 203 and 205 in the background. *Aerospatiale*

Below:
Major Concorde assemblies were delivered to the production lines in Filton and Toulouse by Super Guppy bulk transport conversions of Stratocruisers. *BAC*

Top right:
The major portions of Concorde 214 ready for assembly. *BAC*

Bottom right:
A pair of production Concordes nearing completion at Filton. *BAC*

3 Testing Concorde

Anglo-French technical collaboration first showed tangible results with the unveiling and roll-out of the French-assembled Concorde 001 F-WTSS at Toulouse on 11 December 1967. A thousand guests had assembled for the ceremony, representing the British and French governments, the Concorde customer airlines, the manufacturers and the major subcontractors. At the moment of unveiling the vast upward-hinging hangar door at Toulouse rose to present the sleek white aircraft against a blue backcloth on which were mounted the insignia of the 16 customer airlines, flanked by the Union Flag and the Tricolour. Introductory speeches were made by M Maurice Papon, President of Sud Aviation, and Sir George Edwards, Managing Director of BAC. The governments were represented by M Jean Chamant, French Minister of Transport, followed by Mr Anthony Wedgwood Benn, British Minister of Technology. In his roll-out speech, Mr Benn praised industrial collaboration, encouraged Concorde production, and finally conceded the 'e' in the spelling.

This first public appearance gave the world, in particular the British and French taxpayers, its first chance to appreciate the aircraft in true dimensions. However, there was still a considerable amount of work to be done including detailed checks and ground testing before the Western world's first supersonic airliner was ready for its

maiden flight. These ground tests dragged on amidst false rumours and delays of the impending initial flight. During this time of hard work, and often frustration, the Soviet Tu-144 became the world's first supersonic airliner to take to the air on 31 December 1968. It bore an overall resemblance to Concorde, and accusations have been made in the past about industrial espionage. The slim delta was the best overall answer but the Russian aircraft differed in a number of significant details, which finally resulted in it being abandoned from airline service.

However, just over four years after the first metal had been cut, the Concorde was ready to take to the air. On Saturday, 1 March 1969, the weather was too foggy, but on the following morning, despite continuing mist, the chances appeared better. As the sun warmed up, so the mist was burnt away and announcements were made to the assembled press and the large waiting crowd, that the crew was on board the aircraft and running through the pre-flight checks. The four Olympus engines were started up in turn with the fire trucks and rescue wagons in attendance. Special siren-equipped vehicles rushed along the runway to scare away the large flocks of birds to avoid possible damage to the aircraft. Concorde rolled forward and slowly taxied along the perimeter track on to the threshold of the main runway.

For what seemed an age, the final take-off checks were made, before the engines were

Concorde prototype 001 in the final assembly stage at Toulouse. *Sud-Aviation*

opened up to full power and the brakes released. Slowly picking up speed, the Concorde lifted into the air for the first time, piloted by Andre Turcat, Director of Flight Test for Aerospatiale. The flight was made at a gross weight of 250,000lb (113,500kg) and take-off distance was 4,900ft (1,500m). The maximum altitude reached was 10,000ft (3,050m) and a speed of 250kt (463km/hr) was attained. The droop nose was not raised on this flight, but the undercarriage was raised and lowered normally. The Concorde was accompanied by a Meteor NF11 chaseplane and an MS Paris carrying photographers.

The aircraft returned to the circuit and made its characteristic approach with drooped nose held high, touching the runway 28 minutes after departure. Reverse thrust was engaged, and to assist braking a tail parachute unfurled behind the aircraft. The only incident had been a spurious tail parachute jettison warning, and Turcat's comment was that the aircraft had handled better than the simulator had predicted.

The turn of the British-assembled prototype 02 G-BSST for its first flight came only a month later, on 9 April 1969. As at Toulouse, the Filton airfield at Bristol was surrounded by large crowds eager to see the aircraft, and the press was out in strength.

Despite having been lengthened to 9,000ft (2,743m) for the earlier Brabazon airliner, the Filton runway was too short for the full range of test flying for Concorde. The RAF base of Fairford, Glos, 50 miles (80.5km) to the northeast, had been selected for the flight development programme, and it was here that Brian Trubshaw, Director of Flight Test for BAC's Commercial Air-

craft Division, and his crew landed the aircraft after 42 minutes block time. The aircraft had reached 8,000ft (2,438m) and 280kt (519km/hr) and was essentially similar to the French-assembled 001.

Both aircraft were demonstrated at the Paris Air Show at Le Bourget in June 1969, and on 1 October on its 45th flight Concorde 001 first exceeded Mach 1 for nine minutes at 36,000ft (10,970m). Following modifications, including some to the flying controls, variable geometry intake control system and the installation of more powerful Olympus engines, 002 went supersonic for the first time on 25 March 1970. Concorde 002 was expected to make the first flight to Mach 2 on 4 November 1970, but at Mach 1.35 at 39,000ft (11,895m) a fire warning was indicated in No 2 engine, necessitating a precautionary return to base. 001 had already been scheduled to fly to Mach 2 later the same day, and did so successfully for 53min at 50,200ft (15,300m). 002 caught up on 12 November and flew to the highest altitude to date on New Year's Day 1971 by reaching 57,700ft (17,600m) in a Mach 2 cruise climb.

It was originally foreseen that the flight testing would be shared among seven Concordes; the two prototypes, the two pre-production models and the first three production aircraft. The first major part of the programme was devoted to development flying, to prove the design and to establish the performance characteristics of the airframe, engines and systems. Having established the broad parameters and

investigated the full flight envelope, work commenced on the certification flying, to prove the aircraft safe in normal commercial operation. Included in this was route-proving and endurance flying, to demonstrate that the aircraft could be operated by a normal airline crew and carry fare-paying passengers in comfort.

The first four aircraft were purely test flying laboratories, each one carrying up to 12 tons of test instrumentation, much of it specially developed for Concorde. The two prototypes were only broadly representative of the final production standard, with insufficient range and payload capability to cross the North Atlantic. The pre-production aircraft with their larger fuselages were much closer to the production standard aircraft, with an all-up weight of 340,000lb (154,224kg) and a seating capacity of 139 passengers at a 34in (0.86m) pitch. To obtain this increase in capacity, the fuselage was lengthened by 6.5ft (1.98m) and the rear pressure bulkhead moved aft by 15.67ft (4.78m). A total volumetric payload of 28,000lb (12,700kg) was offered, an increase of 4,400lb (1.996kg) over the prototype payload. The wing areas had not changed, but

performance and operating economics were improved by subtle changes in the wing shape.

Transport aircraft benefit over combat aircraft in their testing phase by having room in the fuselage for flight observers to monitor the behaviour of the aircraft and its systems, as well as room for the instrumentation. In Concorde this instrumentation was capable of recording up to 3,000 different parameters, including pressures, temperatures, accelerations and attitudes, all of which were recorded on magnetic tape for later analysis on the ground. Certain basic information was telemetered to ground monitoring stations during flight, to help analyse any problems or emergency which may occur.

The two flight test centres at Toulouse and Fairford were split broadly in their responsibilities, reflecting the national design tasks. The French led in the handling qualities and the British were responsible for performance. It was a measure of good progress being made in the flight testing that four airline captains, one each from BOAC, Air France, Pan Am and TWA flew Concorde 001 in November 1969. Their flight followed two training sorties on the Toulouse simulator, each pilot reaching Mach 1.2 and being free to try any of the types of failure that had been investigated to date. They found the aircraft pleasant to fly and offering no particular problems to prospective airline pilots and engineers.

Concorde had a unique control problem associated with its high speed, which had to be overcome in a special way. Any swept wing, when flying close to the speed of sound, experiences changes in pressure pattern over it. This has the effect of moving the centre of lift rearward as the speed increases. The result is a tendency for the nose to pitch down, which is

Right:
Concorde 002 G–BSST made its maiden flight from Filton to Fairford on 9 April 1969. *BAe*

Inset:
Brian Trubshaw (left), Chief Test Pilot of BAC at Filton and John Cockrane played a major part in the Concorde flight development programme. *BAC*

corrected by an upward movement of the elevator, or in many cases trimming the whole tailplane. At twice the speed of sound the problem is magnified, with the centre of lift moving back on Concorde about 6ft (2m), which requires a considerable control movement to overcome. To correct this pitch down with the elevons would give an unacceptable increase in drag, and would reduce the remaining available movement for normal aircraft control. To overcome these problems it was decided to make the fuel do the work by installing additional trim tanks, ahead of the main wing tanks and in the extreme tail. The majority of Concorde's 95 tons (96,526kg) of fuel is kept in the main wing tanks, but up to 33 tons (33,530kg) can be used for trimming. As the aircraft accelerates towards Mach 1, the trimming fuel is pumped out of the forward tanks, to collector tanks in the outer wing and the trim tank in the tail, moving the centre of gravity back to balance the change in the centre of lift. At the end of the high speed cruise, when the aircraft is returning to subsonic flight, the fuel is pumped to the forward tank. This fuel trim system gives the bonus of improved control without causing extra drag. Another bonus found was that if on take-off or landing the centre of gravity is moved further back than it need be, the elevons have to be lowered slightly to keep the aircraft in trim. This had the overall effect of increasing the camber of the wing, or producing more lift at low speed giving a very desirable flap effect.

The overall flight development programme involving the seven aircraft was expected to need a total of 4,230 flying hours. This allowed 1,935 for development, 795 for certification and 1,500 for route proving. Because of the sonic boom problem much of the test flying was done over the sea, either in a race track pattern, from the Irish Sea to the Bay of Biscay, or over the North Sea from the north of Scotland down to East Anglia. However, for some supersonic performance testing it was necessary to have a straight line route of 800 miles (1,287km), with the safeguard for the crew and aircraft of continuous radar surveillance and within the range of rescue services. The route chosen to comply with these requirements, yet disturb the minimum number of people, was a north-south line running over the western coasts of Scotland, Wales and Cornwall. It was made quite clear that these were essential

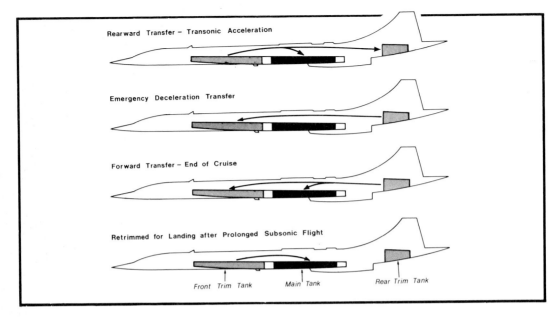

Rearward Transfer – Transonic Acceleration

Emergency Deceleration Transfer

Forward Transfer – End of Cruise

Retrimmed for Landing after Prolonged Subsonic Flight

Front Trim Tank   Main Tank   Rear Trim Tank

Modes of in-flight fuel transfer. *Bob Downey*

test flights, and that not more than 50 could occur over the several years of test flying. Warning was given of these flights, and the government said it would consider any claims for damage caused. These flights caused much criticism, and a number of damage claims were submitted, even after a flight had been scheduled and then cancelled!

To achieve the desired cruising speed of Mach 2, the two critical features to be tested were the successful operation of the engine air intake geometry and also the resistance of the aircraft to a phenomena known as flutter. Any other testing could be fitted around these vital tasks.

The major purpose of the flight test programme was to confirm that the design features, developed in theory, worked in practice. The aircraft had to achieve its predicted performance and be safe. In such an inexact science as aerodynamics, adjustments are always necessary and knowledge is being gained continually. The perfect designer's aircraft would never be built, let alone fly, as there is a continuous flow of new knowledge coming in, and a halt has to be called to allow metal to be cut and at least construct something which will start the programme. Modifications can always be introduced, but that is where the costs begin to escalate, and Concorde was more susceptible to this than other aircraft, due to its pioneering of the unknown and the short production run. In the case of Concorde there were major differences between the prototype, pre-production and production aircraft, resulting in a certain amount of duplication of effort, but the early aircraft proved the basic

product, allowing the fine tuning to be built in later. It was also possible to use the first full scale aircraft to check the validity of the design predictions, giving more accurate estimates for the configuration of the production aircraft.

Amongst the many tests in a flight development programme is stall testing. Although in airline service a stall should never be encountered, should it happen inadvertently the aircraft must be designed to behave 'predictably', and be recoverable as quickly as possible. Concorde however does not stall in the conventional sense, but at low speed can develop a very high sink rate, which is just as dangerous as stalling. As in all modern airliners, a stall warning has been fitted, to alert the crew of the approach to a dangerously low speed. This takes the form of a stick shaker, followed by a more violent vibration if the initial warning is ignored.

Another potentially hazardous situation predicted by the simulator was that the loss of power of one engine at around Mach 1.7 could cause violent loss of control. The gearing of the inner pair of elevons was changed to cope with this problem, which in practice was found to be nonexistent.

As part of the development programme, and to help sell the concept of Concorde, overseas demonstration flights were included at a relatively early stage, the test flying being shared with the manufacturers' test pilots and the airworthiness authority pilots. The airworthiness pilots split their task between testing and certification, allowing a progressive approach to the safety aspects of the aircraft. Another reason for involving the certification pilots at an early stage was to allow them to formulate practical requirements, since Concorde was also well in advance of their knowledge. Following an intense flutter testing programme and other aerodynamic testing, the French prototype 001 made the first intercontinental flight from Toulouse to Dakar on 25 May 1971, its 142nd flight, returning the next day.

Although the overseas flights were not relevant to the direct technical development of the aircraft, they showed it would fit into the contemporary air traffic environment, and provided good public relations. It also gave essential new information on the meteorological conditions at high altitude, where temperature in particular had a significant effect on the operation of the aircraft. Concorde normally cruises between 55,000ft (16,764m) and 60,000ft (18,288m). Over the equator, because the air at the earth's surface is warmer, it rises with greater energy. Rising air cools at about 2°C every 1,000ft (305m) until it reaches the

Right:
The development Concordes had a considerable amount of test instrumentation and recording equipment fitted into the cabin. *BAe*

Below:
Pre-production Concorde 01 G-AXDN in the systems installation phase at Filton. *BAC*

Above:
Concorde 01 G-AXDN testing the anti-spin parachute, by using it for braking at Filton. *BAe*

Above right:
French pre-production Concorde 02 F-WTSA, now preserved at Orly Airport, Paris. *Aerospatiale*

Right:
Concordes 001, 002 and 01 on the tarmac at the Flight Test Centre at Fairford. *BAC*

tropopause, which over the equator is around 55,000ft (16,764m). Therefore the air is much colder than at the same height in temperate latitudes and over the poles, where the tropopause is at only 25,000ft (7,620m). Because the Olympus engines are air-breathing, colder denser air produces more thrust, allowing Concorde to reach its maximum height of 60,000ft (18,288m) much quicker, whereas on the transatlantic route it seldom exceeds 57,000ft (17,375m).

The overseas trips were a unique feature of prototype flying, and demonstrated a very high level of reliability, despite the advanced nature of the aircraft. Prototype 002 made a one-month tour of Asia, departing and returning on schedule.

As already mentioned, flutter testing was a major part of the flight development programme. Flutter is a potentially catastrophic high-frequency vibration of a part of an aircraft structure which can occur if the member is not stiff enough to damp out the flexing effect of a transient aerodynamic shock. The aircraft therefore has to have its resistance to flutter tested by deliberately inducing vibrations into the airframe during flight, to study the response of the structure. In the case of Concorde, the most critical phase was expected to be in the transonic regime, but no problems were encountered.

Few emergencies were experienced during the test programme, but during the display routine practice for Farnborough with 002 in August 1974 a violent structural impact was felt with two loud bangs, as the undercarriage was lowered for landing at Fairford. The undercarriage indicators showed green lights for the nose wheel, starboard main gear and tail bumper, but the port main gear did not appear locked down. The undercarriage was inspected by viewing through the free-fall hatch in the cabin floor, which showed that the main side stay and main retraction jack were completely detached from the main leg. This meant that the leg was totally unsupported. Preparations were made for an emergency landing at Fairford, with the fuel reduced to a minimum. Every effort was made to keep the load off the damaged leg and the brake parachute was deployed to keep the speed down. Some reverse thrust was also used to reduce braking strain on the undercarriage and the aircraft came to a safe halt within the first 5,500ft (1,675m) of the runway. On inspection, the aircraft's weight was found to be only just supported by its undercarriage. As well as the known damage to the port main leg, the starboard one was found to be almost as bad, but still partially restrained by a side stay. It was found that the pin attaching the side strut to the main leg had failed under the additional loads of lowering the undercarriage while the aircraft was turning. Suitable modifications were made to avoid a repeat of this failure.

Another potential hazard was engine surging which, like engine cuts at high mach number, could result in control difficulties or even damage. An American B-58 Hustler had been lost when one engine failed at Mach 2; Concorde had to operate without hazard to its occupants or people under the flight path. The surge problem was demonstrated dramatically on 26 January 1971 when the French prototype 001 was on a test flight over the Atlantic off the southern coast of

Ireland. Tests were being carried out at Mach 1.98 with reheat on engines 1 and 3. When the reheat was shut down the aircraft was subject to violent vibrations, which made the instruments difficult to read. The engine instruments showed no abnormal readings, but the master warning system showed a rapid succession of transient warnings appearing at random on all four engines. On investigation, it was found that No 3 engine had oversped and surged on shut down of the reheat, which caused No 4 to surge as well. The surge was so violent that it blew out the forward intake ramp, damaging the lower lip, and causing internal damage to No 4 engine by ingested metal. After deceleration to Mach 1.2, when all appeared normal again, abortive attempts were made to relight No 4 engine. Examination by periscope revealed damage to the intake, so a return was made to Toulouse on three engines at subsonic speed. No 3 engine had also sustained

damage to its entry guide vanes and compressor blades, but all had been contained within the engines, an essential safety requirement. Modifications were introduced, by alterations in the controls and structural strengthening of the intake ramp, to ensure that if surge did occur damage did not result.

A special test programme was mounted on the British prototype 002 to induce surge deliberately during flight investigation, allowing a thorough analysis and cure for the problem. As a result, the wing leading edge profile was changed to avoid the underwing vortices spilling into the intake, and a more refined control was given to the intake ramp. The aim was to smooth the airflow as much as possible, improve control of the engine variable nozzle and impose practical operational limitations. The surge in fact pushes a large pressure wave out of the intake, which can easily be absorbed by a robust engine, but can cause damage to

flight envelope and caused no damage or loss of control.

In a four-year test programme, surge was eventually banished from the area of flight in which Concorde would normally operate. This operational flight envelope was defined by maximum speed, altitude, mach number and temperature, but still the aircraft had to be tested outside this area to provide adequate safety margins.

As part of the Concorde type certification it was necessary to demonstrate that the aircraft would not encounter any unforeseen problems when operated as a normal airliner. This was the route-proving endurance part of the programme conducted jointly on production aircraft by the launch airlines and their respective manufacturers. One of the features of this part of the programme was that full cabin service was provided for the invited passengers. Aerospatiale and Air France flew aircraft 203 over their proposed North and South Atlantic routes, while BAC and British Airways used 204 for the North Atlantic, Middle East and Asian routes. A total of 755 hours was flown by the aircraft on this programme, the remainder of the 1,000 hours being flown by the development aircraft.

One difficulty encountered on these flights was with the autopilot. The problem was concerned with cruising at Mach 2 at high altitudes because, as mentioned previously, temperature has a critical effect on mach number. Particularly during the endurance flying in Asia where the tropopause is high, any sudden change in temperature caused the aircraft to act quite violently with high rates of climb or descent to

the light and comparatively flimsy intake structure. Not only is there explosive pressure during a surge, but once again flutter can be induced, causing structural damage.

Before the damaging surge on the French prototype, Brian Trubshaw had experienced a multiple surge while flying 002 up to Mach 2 on 12 November 1970 on the specially designated west coast test route. On throttling back from Mach 2 all four engines had surged, causing loud bangs, a great deal of vibration and the entry of smoke into the flight deck through the air conditioning system. The violence of such an occurrence could not be ignored. On 14 April 1974, the British pre-production Concorde was being flown at Mach 2.23 up to 60,000ft (18,288m) from Tangier, when surges occurred at Mach 2.20 on cancellation of reheat. These surges occurred outside the normal operating

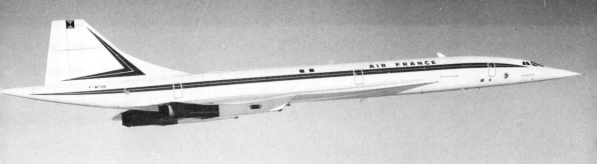

Concorde 201 F-WTSB in the old Air France livery.
Aerospatiale

maintain its set mach number. As the aircraft climbed, the temperature changed again, causing a chain reaction, and mach number variations could be from 1.9 to 2.1. A solution had to be found for this uncomfortable situation: a speed hold of 530kt (964.5km/hr) was made until Mach 2 was reached when a combined hold was introduced, and damping from accelerometers was provided to avoid violent manoeuvres. If the mach number was rising too rapidly, the auto-throttles automatically reduced power to take the energy out of the aircraft. This also avoided inadvertently exceeding Mach 2, which could otherwise be passed at the initial cruising height of 50,000ft (15,240m), where Mach 2 and the maximum operating speed of 530kt (964.5km/hr) intersect, and the aircraft still had an excess of energy and acceleration.

Some long delays were caused in the British endurance flying operations due to the need for five engine changes on Concorde 204 because of a combustion chamber fault, and an undercarriage leg change in the open air at Bahrain. Unlike normal airline operations, there was no back-up aircraft. This endurance testing complemented the many overseas demonstration flights flown by the prototypes. On 4 September 1971 Concorde 001 flew a 15-day tour of South America, visiting Rio de Janeiro, Sao Paulo and Buenos Aires. Nearly 100 South American guests were flown at speeds up to Mach 2, and the aircraft fitted into the airport traffic patterns, even in the adverse weather experienced on a number of occasions.

It was in 1971 that the end came to the still-born rival American SST. The US Senate voted to end funding in March, much of the 'credit' for this decision going to the environmental lobby. The main causes of the design's demise were technical and financial. The elimination of this prospective competition was in general regarded as bad news by the European Concorde builders, who would have preferred to see a complementary American SST following behind, to avoid having to fight all the political battles with Concorde alone.

Despite some misgivings, including amongst some of the people directly involved in the Concorde programme who found it hard to imagine that a supersonic airliner could be certificated to carry over 100 people at Mach 2 for three hours across the Atlantic, the aircraft proved its worth. It flew exceptionally well, helped by its fly-by-wire controls and systems which gave it exactly the right level of stability and control. However, where Concorde really proved itself was that if all the special systems and air data computers were switched off at Mach 2, it was still safely controllable in manual reversion. The pilot was then directly flying Concorde through mechanical

Concorde 202 G-BBDG on approach to Fairford. *BA*

British Airways Concorde 204 G-BOAC made its maiden flight from Filton 27 February 1975. The vortex lift has created water vapour on the wing top surface. *BA*

linkage, and it could be brought in to land safely with no real problems. The main concern was the manual operation of the variable intakes above Mach 1.6, but there was adequate instrumentation to assist in this case.

Up to Concorde Type Certification, the total flight time was 5,495 hours, of which development took 37%, certification 18% and endurance flying 17%. The remaining 28% consisted mainly of training, demonstrations, transit flying, official flights and tours. A special category Certificate of Airworthiness was issued to Concorde 204 G-BOAC on 30 June 1975, to allow the aircraft to carry non-paying passengers on the route-proving flights. The type certification for the Rolls-Royce/ SNECMA Olympus 593 Mk 610-14-28 engine was awarded jointly by the British and French authorities on 29 September 1975. On 9 October the French issued a 'Certificat de Navigabilité' in Paris for Concorde, followed on 5 December by the Aircraft Type Certificate by the British Civil Aviation Authority. The delay between the two had been caused by checks on autopilot modifications, introduced as result of the temperature variations experienced during route proving.

The airworthiness authorities continue to monitor progress and behaviour in operation, including modifications to overcome any additional problems experienced in airline operation. In November 1978 British Airways Concordes were cleared to land automatically in bad weather conditions covered by Category 3 weather conditions. This allowed landings to be made under automatic control, down to a decision height of 15ft (4.5m) above the ground and a visibility of 820ft (250m) at the threshold. As had happened all the way through the programme, the Anglo-French accord did not coincide. The French airworthiness authorities had cleared the Air France Concordes for autoland 12 months previously, but to a decision height of 35ft (10.7m) and 656ft (200m) for the runway visual range.

Concorde could now start to prove itself in service and hopefully begin to earn some return on the massive investment. The total development cost shared between the two countries was £1,134million, none of which could be recovered on the modest number of sales. Production costs combined for the two countries reached £654million, of which £278million was recovered from the airlines. Meanwhile, the American taxpayers had spent more than $1,035million on the research, design, development, tests, studies and mock-ups of their abortive supersonic airliner programme. For about the same as Britain's share in Concorde development up to certification, America had failed to produce an aircraft.

4 Concorde Power – the Olympus Engine

Power for Concorde came from four Rolls-Royce/SNECMA Olympus 593 Mk 610 engines, developed from the Bristol Olympus engines produced for the cancelled TSR2 low level strike bomber, which had originally been developed from the earlier Olympus engines which powered the Vulcan V-Bomber. Together, they produced 152,200lb (69,040kg) of thrust for take-off and 27,160lb (12,320kg) of thrust in Mach 2 cruise at 60,000ft (18,288m).

The power choice required an engine capable of successful operation throughout a wide range of flight conditions. High thrust was needed for take-off, transonic acceleration, and long periods of supersonic cruise. Low fuel consumption was required for supersonic cruise and the subsonic parts of the flight, which were substantially over land. A turbo-fan engine offered the best specific fuel economy, but it needed a much higher mass flow of air to provide the required thrust, and therefore would be much larger and heavier. To keep the cross section, and therefore drag, to a minimum a pure jet was the best answer, and the high jet velocity of a low bypass engine was necessary, otherwise the exhaust velocity itself would tend to slow the aircraft. The pure jet moves a smaller mass of air faster, but has the disadvantage of producing far greater noise as the high speed exhaust mixes with the otherwise static air.

In the case of a supersonic transport, the engine is only one of three major elements of the powerplant and its installation within the overall airframe is absolutely critical. Mention has already been made of the all-important variable geometry air intake ahead of the engine, and the equally important propelling nozzles at the rear. As would be expected, at take-off the engine is providing the major power source, but this is only 82% of the total, the intake contributing 21% and the nozzles 6%. The extra 9% is accounted for by intake drag. In supersonic cruise the effect is more dramatic, with the engine contributing 8% of the thrust, the intake providing 75% and the nozzles 29%. The intake drag accounts for the additional 12%. The intake operation is therefore critical to successful supersonic cruise, with the nozzle playing a major part. With the intake, full control must be maintained of temperatures, pressures and engine compressor speeds, controlling the power throughout the widely varying flight conditions. No jet engine can accept air at its compressors at supersonic speeds. In the most difficult case it is necessary to slow the air down from Mach 2 to Mach 0.5 before allowing it to enter the engine. This is achieved over the 11ft (3.35m) length of intake, which has the desirable effect of compressing it, to help the engines' own

The Rolls-Royce Olympus engine for Concorde on the test bed at Patchway near Bristol. *Rolls-Royce*

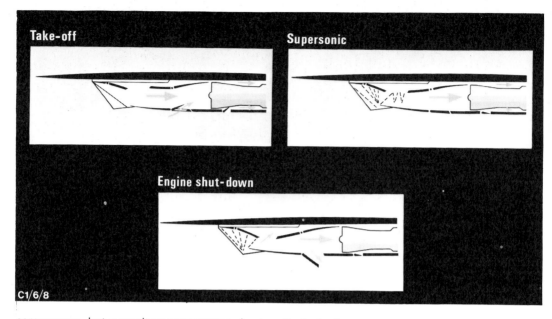

Take-off

Supersonic

Engine shut-down

C1/6/8

Engine intake cross-section. *BAe*

compressors, but a resultant temperature rise to about 200°C creates the need for special metals in the construction of the engine. At take-off the engines requires the maximum air, so the intake ramps are fully up and additional air is allowed in through the auxiliary doors on the underside of the nacelle. As transonic speeds are approached, the auxiliary doors are closed and above Mach 1.3 the ramps lower to create a series of shock waves, starting from the bottom lip of the intake. As the aircraft moves along it meets changes in air temperature and pressure, which have to be compensated for by fine adjustments of the intake ramps. Any changes in engine power require intake changes, which is dealt with by the computing system. In the case of shut-down or failure, the engine suddenly needs no air at all, and in this difficult case the ramps divert some of the air over the top of the engine and much of the remainder is dumped out of the underside spill door. The rapid operation of this system is critical; and as proof in testing the slam-closure of a throttle at Mach 2 made the engine react, but the aircraft remained quite docile.

To achieve this sophisticated control of the powerplant required the employment of some advanced technology. A high level of accuracy had to be obtained, and when dealing with the inexact science of aerodynamics this was quite a challenge. The French had developed an analogue control system for the prototype aircraft, but there were very grave doubts as to whether it would be accurate enough for the production aircraft. The system depended upon so-called 'magic holes', which took measurements at critical points, to be used in the control process. The French had done

a tremendous amount of work on this system, and despite its shortcomings did not want to discard it. However, so much information was required in the vicinity of the engine intake, that the 'magic holes' could not be relied upon. The atmosphere was quite naturally disturbed by the aircraft, and this, combined with measuring inaccuracies, resulted in an unacceptable situation for the computer. The alternative was to accept the best quality inputs available, although less detailed, and process them in a much more sophisticated and accurate manner by digital means. Although this method produced the desired results, the development costs were higher than estimated, due to the lack of previous experience. To achieve the necessary high safety levels, only the best quality components were used, and due to the high reliability required, delays were experienced in achieving the programme.

Olympus cruise performance was very much as estimated eight years earlier, but the expected take-off and transonic performance had not been achieved. Fortunately, reheat came to the rescue for these critical flight conditions, and despite the dramatic increase in fuel consumption, it was considered acceptable to attain the more economical cruising speed as rapidly as possible. As the aircraft weight increased, an extra stage was added to the front of the low-pressure compressor and the blades were cooled to allow high operating temperatures. About half-way through the development programme, another significant change was made. The original 'cannular' combustion chamber was changed in favour of an

'annular' vaporising chamber, which not only saved weight, but cleaned up Concorde's smoky exhaust.

As well as the variable air intake, the other highly critical part of the powerplant was the nozzle. In order to be capable of carrying a payload, Concorde had to have a jet pipe which first compressed the exhaust gases in a convergent nozzle, and then expanded them again through a divergent nozzle. It was also necessary to be able to vary the cross section of the primary convergent nozzle to extract the best performance from the engine across the full range of flight conditions, and to allow precise control. To produce the best nozzle proved to be one of the most difficult parts of the powerplant development, three types being tried before the best compromise between efficiency, drag, reverse thrust and weight was obtained. Reverse thrust was achieved by a pair of 'clam shell' doors hinged at the rear of the jet pipe. On take-off they were closed slightly, allowing air to be sucked in from the outside for mixing with the exhaust. This helped to reduce noise, as well as improving engine performance. As speed increased they opened progressively to become part of the divergent nozzle. On landing all four clam shell doors were closed, deflecting the jet forward above and below the wings to provide reverse thrust for braking. The two inboard clam shells could be used in the air to increase the rate of descent.

The Bristol Olympus is a two-spool engine, which consists of low-pressure and high-pressure compressors each driven by its own turbines. In addition to the intake ramp and nozzle controls,

Preparations for a test run of a Rolls-Royce Olympus 593 engine on the test bed at Bristol. *Rolls-Royce*

there is also control of the fuel flow using the pilot's throttle levers which determine the speed of the high-pressure compressor. The low-pressure turbine is controlled by the variable nozzle. Additionally, there is the reheat system where additional fuel is sprayed into the hot exhaust gases, to boost the dry thrust when necessary.

To manage the fuel system for engine control over the wide range of temperatures, it was decided to have a simple hydromechanical pumping and flow control, with the difficult controlling functions handled electronically. This was to allow modification easily, by simple change of electronics, avoiding massive mechanical modifications. Changes could even be made overnight and between flights each day. The Concorde engine control system was analogue, because at the time of its design, digital technology was not sufficiently advanced. An experimental digital control system was flown on Concorde at the latter part of the development, but by then the analogue system components had already been delivered.

The engine control system, linked with the autopilot, is fully automatic from take-off to touch down, the pilot simply selecting throttles fully open and switching to each mode of flight. He does however exercise some manual control on taxying at slightly above idle power, and he reduces power after take-off to reduce noise in the initial climb.

In developing the Olympus engines for Concorde, every time the weight of the aircraft

Left, top to bottom:

The Vulcan B Mk 1 XA903 Olympus engine flying test bed had a water spray rig fitted in front of the crew entry door for icing tests on the engine. *Rolls-Royce*

The Rolls-Royce Olympus 593 engine intakes on Air France Concorde F-BVFA. *Philip Birtles*

The jet exhausts with reverse thrust cascades on Air France Concorde F-BVFA at New York. *Philip Birtles*

Right:

Concorde G-BBDG 202 taking off with undercarriage retracting. Each Rolls-Royce Olympus engine is carefully located to reduce airflow problems; note the wide spacing of the engine nacelles. *BAe*

increased, or fuel consumption went up, the engine builders had to squeeze just a little more performance out of their product, to maintain the marginal transatlantic range capability.

A number of ground-based test rigs were used to develop, in particular, the interaction between the intake and the engine. Wind tunnel models were used to determine air pressure and velocity patterns, which were reproduced on a full scale rig, giving a simulation of the aircraft stationary on the ground. In Cell 4 at the National Gas Turbine Establishment at Pyestock, flight conditions were simulated for the intake/engine combination.

An Avro Vulcan B Mk 1, XA903, was modified to carry an Olympus 593 under its belly in a representative nacelle, as a subsonic test-bed for the engine flying on 9 September 1966, and flew with a definitive Olympus 593-3B on 3 November 1969. This installation was removed by Marshalls of Cambridge, after the aircraft was flown there on 4 August 1971. It was on this Vulcan that the engine electrical control system was developed.

When the designers had solved the problem of fitting the engines closely in the nacelles, it was found nearly impossible to service them without removal. The whole of the outside of the engine had to be redesigned to give access for maintenance. The technology of engine inspection was also advanced on Concorde, where internal inspections could be made, to anticipate possible failure. Inspection holes were provided in the engine casing to allow internal probe inspections between flights. Magnetic plugs were installed in the oil circuits, to pick-up specks of metal and warn of bearing failures.

A potentially dangerous mechanical problem identified with Concorde's Olympus engines, was the possibility of a shaft breaking. A TSR2 engine had suffered this problem and destroyed its test-bed Vulcan, fortunately on the ground. The cause had been a temperature difference in the shaft as the engine cooled after shut-down, leaving the top warmer than the bottom. When the engine was restarted and power increased, the additional strain on the shaft had caused it to break. The simple solution for Concorde's engines was a slow rotation to even out temperatures before restarting.

Other mechanical problems were caused by the exceptionally high operating temperatures of the engine requiring the use of special and expensive metals such as titanium and nickel-alloy blades, and special lubricants had to be developed to work at about 200°C. The engines were produced to a very demanding and tight specification, leaving little chance of significant improvement during their development programme to give the airframe builder his usual performance bonus.

Another problem was the installation of the engine package on the aircraft. All four intakes had to be physically different, because the effect of swept leading edge meant that the engine pairs were 'toed-in' at a slight angle. The aerodynamics of the wing were slightly different at the outboard and inboard nacelles, and all four intakes differed slightly, to adapt to the air flow. With the engines rotating all in the same direction, the aerodynamic conditions of each engine differed slightly. The alternative of 'handed' rotation was not acceptable due to spares and interchangeability problems. It was obviously a difficult development problem to absorb the aerodynamic differences, particularly as when the aircraft manoeuvred it was difficult to obtain sufficiently uniform pressure conditions.

Engine surge had already been covered to some extent under the flight testing of Concorde. The problem was a challenge to the engineers and alarming to the test crews — the air intake

Air France Concorde 203 F-WTSC with the variable exhaust nozzles partly deployed. *Air France*

was the critical area for solving this problem. If for any reason the compressed air flow in the intakes went outside the design limitations, then a breakdown in the compression process could occur. This would cause the high-pressure air in the combustion chamber to move forward at a very high velocity, creating a pressure wave and an explosive effect. If not corrected, the engine could go into continuous cyclic surge conditions. However, despite all the noise and vibration caused by a surge, the engines normally suffered no ill-effects. After a surge an engine usually continued to run, but if not it could easily be relit.

In the first nine months of passenger service British Airways reached 3,800 engine operating hours on Concordes 204 and 206, with only two unscheduled removals. Air France had flown 7,600 hours on four aircraft in the same time, and had no shutdowns in the first 5,000 hours. Both airlines were happy with the service entry, the Olympus giving better reliability than the big fan engines at a similar stage in their service, despite more flight cycles due to a greater emphasis on

crew training. As a precaution British Airways positioned two spare engines at Bahrain before starting to fly the route, but as there were no calls on spares one of the units was returned to Heathrow.

The unplanned engine removals mentioned were largely due to the passive nature of the snags experienced, allowing services to continue until a suitable opportunity arose for rectification, avoiding engine changes away from base. Even three-engine ferry flights were quite practical. Initial unplanned engine removal rate was just over one per 1,000 engine hours, half of the removals being due to unacceptably high oil consumption.

The engine consisted of 12 modules including the afterburner, and borescope inspection of the most critical items was made every 1,250 operating hours. The engine oil was analysed spectrographically every 25 hours to monitor engine wear at the earliest stage. The magnetic chip detectors on each engine, located in the gear box drives, were examined every 75 hours.

The initial specific fuel consumption was better than the guarantees and great care had to be taken to avoid deterioration in efficiency due to engine age. Any small increase in consumption, due to wear or inaccurate fuel management, can have a serious effect on range or payload capability.

The Olympus engines were found to be robust and tolerant to ingestion of foreign objects. No 4 engine had experienced compressor vibration in the development phase due to a vortex caused by the nosegear door reacting with the engine. A switch on the flightdeck inhibited full throttle on that engine below 60kt (111km/hr), decoupling the vortex from the compressor.

Despite the comprehensive flight development programme, averaging 250 hours per engine, it was insufficient to identify a number of problems encountered with the ancillary equipment in service. The main engine first stage fuel pumps were failing prematurely and the electrical connectors in the vicinity of the intakes became unscrewed due to vibration. Wire-locking had no apparent effect, and they had to be inspected and tightened every 25 flying hours. Engine overhaul by British Airways is handled at Treforest, where repairs are undertaken, but the separate modules are changed at the Heathrow engineering base.

The Olympus engines for Concorde therefore had a relatively trouble free and undramatic entry into service, with all the major development problems overcome, leaving a few minor areas of concern on high oil consumption and ancillary reliability. Considering the critical nature of the engine performance to the successful Concorde operations, this was a creditable achievement.

5 Concorde Equipment

Concorde's navigational equipment is fairly conventional and similar in many respects to the Boeing 747, which was entering service at around the same time. It was logical to maintain as much commonality as possible, since Boeing equipment was up to date and spares and maintenance could be pooled. However, Concorde had to be navigated more precisely, particularly to avoid the antisocial effects of the sonic boom on populations close to the flight path. In addition to the normal equipment to allow Concorde to fly on the pre-defined airways, the aircraft was also equipped with three inertial navigation systems (INS), for overwater flight, where the assistance of navigation beacons was not available. Before commencing a flight, the INS is told the starting point in relation to true north and the latitude, and all subsequent movements are dependent on the force of gravity and accelerations of the aircraft. The INS computer calculates any movement and provides the crew with the aircraft position to an accuracy of about one mile (1.6km) every hour of flight. INS is particularly suited to supersonic flight, as speed does not have any effect on the error, and the shorter flight times reduce the margin.

In Concorde, to limit the growth of error, three computers work in parallel to give the best estimated position, to an accuracy of better than half a mile (0.8km) per hour of flight, or about one mile (1.6km) for the whole ocean crossing.

The accuracy of the system is needed most on the initial approach to the coastlines of either southwest Britain or the eastern seaboard of the USA on route to New York and Washington. At this point the use of the traditional navigational aids on the ground bring the aircraft on to its accurate flight path at subsonic speeds.

The Concorde routes are defined by a series of predetermined waypoints, fixed by latitude and longitude at any change of heading. Up to nine of these points can be fed into the computer in advance, and once passed can become available for reprogramming in rotation. To save individual programming on a regular route, pre-programmed card inserts can be used.

Combined with the use of the standard Distance Measuring Equipment (DME) — which provides a radar measurement of distance from known beacons — a high enough standard of navigation for Concorde is achieved by INS. The use of automatic data reduces crew workload, and the accuracy of the data provides the necessary navigational precision. The INS also provides accurate attitude and direction information to the basic flight system and the autopilots.

Compared with the modern wide-bodied jet airliners, the Concorde flight deck appears cramped and crowded. Due to the streamlining of the nose, it is certainly small by modern standards, and much of the wall and roof area is covered by control panels and instrumentation, as well as the space occupied by the pilots' instrument panel itself.

The basic flight instruments are familiar to most pilots, but Concorde has a few new instruments and modifications to the existing ones to take care of the extra performance in the high altitude supersonic regime. In front of him the pilot has airspeed, attitude, altitude, angle of attack, vertical speed, heading, Machmeter, sideslip and navigational aids. In the centre panel between the pilots are the engine controls, undercarriage selection, nose and visor selector and indication of the flight controls' position. On the glare shield are the autopilot and autothrottle controls.

Between the pilots is the control pedestal which contains the three INS controls and displays, the throttles and trim controls, as well as communications. The pilots' side panels contain the nosewheel steering and weather radar.

Above the pilot's heads is a roof panel carrying the controls and switches for the ancillary systems such as lighting, de-icing, engine high pressure fuel cocks, flying control selection, and engine fire extinguisher handles. At the forward part of this roof panel is the master warning panel to identify any failed system. This is usually monitored by the flight engineer on take-off and landing, when he faces forward between the two pilots for these phases of operation. Therefore, although the pilots positions appear cramped they are surrounded by their controls, all of which are within easy reach when required.

The flight engineer has his own systems panel

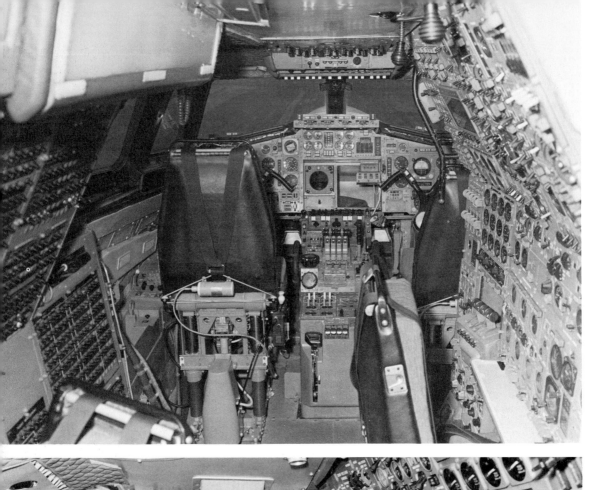

on the starboard side of the cockpit which controls all the major aircraft systems, such as pressurisation, air conditioning, electrical services, engine performance, intake positions, fuel, centre of gravity and engine start. Much of this is operated automatically, but in the event of failure any problems can be monitored and corrected where possible manually, or an alternative system selected.

As with all modern commercial aircraft Concorde is fitted with a sophisticated automatic flight system which is tailored to the handling characteristics of the aircraft. Linked with the autothrottle, the Concorde autopilot has five horizontal and 12 vertical modes, many of them common to other airliners. However, the maximum climb and maximum cruise modes are unique to Concorde, being used to hold the aircraft within the limits of indicated airspeed, Mach number and skin temperature.

As part of the automatic flight system Concorde features an automatic landing capability which not only brings the aircraft into land safely in poor visibility, but when used regularly gives a clearly defined and predictable approach to any destination. This helps air traffic control and relieves some of the crew load at the busiest time, allowing improved and safer overall control.

6 Concorde Into Service

With the Certificate of Airworthiness awarded, the way was clear for Concorde to enter service, following the training of the airline air and ground crews by the manufacturers. The test teams and designers now had to hand over their masterpiece, to be operated by the airlines to earn some revenue. The first delivery was F-BVFA to Air France at Charles de Gaulle airport in Paris on 19 December 1975. By the time the first aircraft for British Airways, G-BOAA, was delivered to Heathrow on 14 January 1976, Air France had already received its second aircraft.

The two airlines agreed to operate their inaugural services simultaneously; British Airways from London to Bahrain as the initial step for the proposed route to Australia, and Air France from Paris to Rio de Janeiro. The date was set for 21 January 1976, and the time at 11.40hrs GMT. It was agreed that should there be any last minute delay with one of the aircraft, the other would wait for up to 20 minutes before departing.

The two control towers at London and Paris were linked by telephone, and the two aircraft captains, Norman Todd and Pierre Chamoine were in touch over the radio during push-back once the engines were started. Both aircraft were in position on their respective runways four minutes before take-off and, following a 30-second countdown, the brakes were released at exactly the same time. This historic departure into airline service carried many passengers comprising a mixture of fare-payers and invited guests, including the Duke of Kent, and a substantial number of press to publicise the Concorde operation to the world. As with the maiden

The first Concorde delivery to British Airways, Concorde 206 G-BOAA arrived at Heathrow 14 January 1976. *BAC*

flights, the airport buildings and perimeters were crowded with enthusiastic spectators, and the roads were jammed with parked cars. In addition, the departure was covered by television, the actual take-offs being shown together on a split screen. It was later estimated that some 250million people around the world watched this event on television.

The British Concorde made a faultless departure turning to the southeast towards Worthing, in a climb of 25,000ft (7,620m). The initial part of the route to the west of Paris, over Geneva and Venice was subsonic to avoid the nuisance of the sonic boom. The transonic check list was started, and 1hr 20min after take-off, the aircraft became supersonic, climbing and accelerating rapidly. Mach 2 was reached at 50,000ft (15,140m) half way down the Adriatic Sea, the aircraft heading towards the Mediterranean and turning left beyond the south of Greece, to pass Cyprus and make a landfall just north of Beirut. Concorde continued supersonically over Syrian airspace at 60,000ft (18.288m), the sun setting abruptly behind the aircraft. The final part of the flight was about 25 miles (40.25km) to the south of the main oil pipeline, the descent commencing 280 miles (450km) from the destination. The touch-down was made at Bahrain at 15.17hrs GMT, 3hr 37min after departure from London.

Meanwhile, Air France Concorde F-BVFA had departed subsonically from Paris until crossing the coast, when it accelerated through the transonic regime to Mach 2 close to the Iberian Peninsula, past the Canary Islands, and off the west coast of Africa to the first landing at Dakar at 14.24hrs GMT. Leaving Dakar at 15.24hrs, there was a minor delay in accelerating through Mach 1

The inaugural Concorde service. G-BOAA 206 departed from Heathrow 21 January 1976 for Bahrain. *BAC*

caused by a secondary air door failing to open and restricting cooling airflow around the engines. However, this problem was overcome and the arrival was made at Rio de Janeiro at 19.05hrs GMT, both flights being totally successful.

The return flights were made the next day, and with the press conference over the aircraft and crews could settle down to their regular schedules. The British Airways route to Bahrain was operationally more demanding than the initial Air France route, because of the accurate tracking and careful planning required particularly when flying supersonically over the Middle Eastern countries. Bahrain was only the first leg of an eventual 13.5-hour route via Singapore to Australia, and was therefore not expected to be all that popular initially. Even so, in the first six months the load factor was 48.5%, double that predicted by the airline, and there was no significant reduction in subsonic traffic. Concorde passengers were prepared to pay the premium of 20% above the first class fare to reach their destination in just over half the normal time. Two return flights per week were scheduled to Bahrain, leaving London at 11.00hrs every Monday and Wednesday. The return was made the following day, departing from Bahrain at 09.45hrs. The one-class passenger cabin contained 100 seats, and this initial schedule called for only 16 flying hours per week.

Air France at least had a final destination to serve, making the start with two round trips per week, leaving Paris at 13.00hrs each Sunday and Wednesday. The return flight left Rio de Janeiro at 20.30hrs the same day, giving a total utilisation of 25 hours each week. Within the first six

months, Air France had added Caracas to its South American destinations.

The first step in extending the British Airways routes to the east was made when a joint BA/Singapore Airlines service was started, extending from Bahrain to Singapore in December 1977. It was halted after three round trips due to an objection by the Malaysian Government to Concorde flying over the Straits of Malacca. After lengthy negotiations, the Bahrain to Singapore operations were resumed on 24 January 1979, but were again withdrawn on 1 November 1980 due to poor load factors which did not cover the cost of operation. The planned extension to Darwin and Sydney, and the other mainly overland routes to Tokyo, and Johannesburg via Lagos were never started.

The key to Concorde's success however was the North Atlantic route to New York, and the Americans were reluctant for environmental reasons to allow the aircraft to land unless it could be proved to be within the noise and pollution limits. The attempts to obtain approval for scheduled Concorde flights to the United States began in February 1975 with letters from the two airlines to Mr Charles Carey, Assistant Administrator for Internal Affairs at the Federal Aviation Administration (FAA) in Washington DC. These letters requested the amendments to the airline's operational specifications to allow regular Concorde flights to New York and Washington to begin in early 1976. This action was regarded by the Americans as something which might significantly affect the quality of the human environment, and required the preparation of an Environmental Impact Statement (EIS), which analysed the impact on the environment, and allowed it to be exposed to public scrutiny if necessary at public hearings. The Anglo-French case was presented jointly by the two airlines, assisted by the two European governments and the four manufacturers responsible for the airframe and engines. (The first technical data on Concorde had been submitted to the FAA in October 1974 to obtain approval for the route-proving part of Concorde flying. The EIS procedure could not be completed in time for the route-proving, and so the latter was rearranged to miss out the USA.)

The application for commercial operations from each airline averaged two flights a day to

New York, and one a day to Washington, the EIS commencing on this basis. In March 1975, a draft EIS was published followed by public FAA hearings in April. On the basis of these comments, a voluminous final EIS was released to the public in November, and Secretary of Transportation, William Coleman fixed 5 January 1976 for the public hearing in Washington. The Anglo-French argument suggested that the limited environmental impact of Concorde services to the United States would be far outweighed by the benefits of the service, together with the important international considerations, economic benefits and technological progress represented by the aircraft. It would be an extraordinary and discriminatory act to exclude six daily Concorde flights to the USA.

After careful deliberation, Secretary Coleman decided to permit British Airways and Air France to conduct limited Concorde scheduled flights into the United States for a trial period not to exceed 16 months. This decision was published on 4 February 1976 and allowed the frequency requested by the two airlines into New York and Washington. Amongst the conditions were that all flights would arrive or depart between 07.00 and 22.00hrs; that operations would normally be from Heathrow or Charles de Gaulle; there was to be no supersonic flying over the United States; and reasonable noise abatement procedures would be imposed.

The key condition was the noise of the Concorde engines, on the approach, landing, and take-off. The FAA had promulgated noise standards for subsonic aircraft, but not supersonic aircraft. It was realised that it would not be possible to reduce the noise impact of Concorde to the levels of the fan engine-powered wide-bodied airliners. Objections came not only because of the noise impact, but also due to the energy used for a relatively small number of people, and the damage to the high level ozone layer which might upset the ecological balance. However, the impact of even the maximum number of SST's flying (including the possibility of the Russian TU-144s) was likely to cause climatic effects too small to be measurable. As far as polluting the environment with carbon monoxide was concerned, the aircraft was far cleaner than the average car. Concorde only discharged 5lb (2.77kg) of pollutant into the air per 1,000 miles (1,609km), as opposed to 50lb (22.70kg) or more of a typical car over the same distance.

The major US airlines, Pan Am and TWA, suggested that Concorde would monopolise the first class passengers on the transatlantic market, making things even more difficult for the financially troubled American flag carriers. It was also seen as a threat to the dominance of the

Left, top to bottom:

Concorde 204 G-BOAC at Bahrain during route proving. *BAC*

Concorde 204 G-BOAC at Singapore mid-1975 during route proving. *BAC*

Concorde 204 G-BOAC departed from London Heathrow Airport 24 May 1976 for the inaugural service to Washington DC. *BAC*

world aviation industry by the US manufacturers.

Favourable reasons for accepting Concorde included international co-operation, technological progress and aviation policy. By halving the time of a transatlantic flight, international trade, commerce and cultural exchange benefited. The United States would be participating in the environmental consequences and commercial viability of Concorde, to judge how a second generation SST might be developed. It would also be in a position to influence international SST standards. To ban Concorde from the United States could cause economic problems in Britain and France, and result in retaliation from Europe.

Returning to the noise problem, four points were taken into consideration. One was the actual measurement of the aircraft noise under and to one side of the approach and take-off paths. Secondly, a single event noise contour was drawn up to show the areas of population subjected to particular noise intensities. The third point was to provide a noise exposure forecast giving a cumulative noise impact of all aircraft operating from an airport during a day. This includes when the noise can be most disturbing and indicate an extra burden of noise, such as Concorde. Finally, an aircraft sound descriptor system measured the cumulative impact, but with emphasis on the total time of exposure to high noise levels.

There was no doubt that Concorde would contribute more noise to the airport environment although it would not be noisier than the current Boeing 707 and Douglas DC-8 airliners which at the time formed over a quarter of the US commercial airline fleet. The small number of Con-

Above:
The Air France and British Airways Concordes made a simultaneous arrival at Washington DC 24 May 1976 and parked nose to nose in front of the futuristic terminal building. *BAe*

Top right:
Concorde 201 F-WTSB made the first visit by the aircraft to New York Kennedy Airport 19 October 1977 to demonstrate its compliance with the stringent noise regulations. *BA*

Bottom right:
The first Concorde commercial service from London to New York was with 206 G-BOAA which departed from London Heathrow Airport 22 November 1977. *BA*

corde flights would make only a marginal additional noise impact around New York's Kennedy Airport and because of the sparse population around Washington's Dulles Airport, the addition of Concorde would be hardly perceptible. Concorde would be making eight movements at Kennedy Airport, out of the grand total of nearly 1,000 daily operations. The 16-month trial period was set, to allow a further review of the operation once sufficient experience had been gained.

The implementation of the Coleman decision at Washington's Dulles Airport was relatively straightforward, as the administration of the airport was by the FAA, which was controlled by the Department of Transportation. However, Kennedy Airport was administered by the Port of New York & New Jersey Authority which was concerned about possible lawsuits against it due to the extra noise, and was reluctant to grant landing rights.

Planning was able to commence for flights to Washington, the inaugural being a simultaneous arrival by Concordes of Air France and British Airways. As a simultaneous landing was too much to expect, it was agreed that the British aircraft would land first, with the Air France aircraft 12 minutes behind crossing the Atlantic, reducing the gap as the airport was approached.

Before the aircraft could commence this service, the airport and air traffic authorities had to be convinced that Concorde could fit into existing traffic patterns. It was pointed out that any help in expediting the air routes would be a welcome saving of fuel. The inbound and outbound routes over the sea had to avoid the hazards of airspace reserved for the testing of military aircraft, causing a major dog-leg over the sea after departing Washington. The inbound route could fly over the top of the warning areas. Because of the various restrictions and unknowns in the operations, British Airways decided to limit the payload on initial operations to 80 passengers on the westbound flights.

The inaugural flight to Dulles was set for 24 May 1976, the British Airways Concorde G-BOAC leading the Air France aircraft across the Atlantic. The weather forecast was good and the usual mixture of occupants included VIPs, press and fare-paying passengers. The descent commenced with Air France close behind, but on the final approach the leading aircraft was slowed to its minimum speed by the controller, due to a light aircraft not responding to instructions. However, it was not an obstruction, and the two Concordes landed two minutes apart. By taxying over different pre-determined routes, the two aircraft came face to face and stopped together in front of the control tower and futuristic terminal building, raising their noses and visors together. The inevitable press conference followed with particular interest in the incident concerning the British Airways Concorde and the light aircraft, which had been possibly carrying press photographers.

The departure of the British Concorde caused some controversy as by chance the aircraft avoided the noise monitors which were set up on a parallel runway. The Air France aircraft had already departed from Runway 19 Left, but the British Airways Concorde Captain chose 19 Right for his departure as the route took the aircraft over fewer communities, and therefore reduced the noise nuisance. Despite some bad press caused by this inadvertent avoidance, the Con-

As at Washington, the Air France and British Airways Concordes made a simultaneous arrival at New York Kennedy Airport 22 November 1977. *BA*

British Airways Concorde 206 G-BOAA at the terminal on arrival after the first commercial service from London to New York 22 November 1977. *BA*

cordes created a good impression and were not considered as undesirable as had been predicted. In fact, most people found the aircraft acceptable, and were at last able to judge the Concorde for themselves.

Successful though Washington had been, the real goal was New York, and there were still problems to be overcome. Air France and British Airways announced their intention to commence flights into Kennedy Airport from 10 April 1976. The Port Authority however responded with a ban on Concorde flights until there had been at least a six-month evaluation period of operations at Washington, London and Paris. The ban was imposed entirely on the grounds of aircraft noise despite the fact that it had never flown into New York. The airlines responded by threatening legal action, but this was delayed as the two national groups were not in agreement over the best course of action. The French suggested that if the legal process was started, and produced the wrong result, it could be irreversible. They preferred to try the more cautious public relations approach, leaving the courts to decide only if that failed. The British were keen to test the ban on Concordes in the courts, as they believed it to be totally illegal, and was bound to be overturned.

With a number of unsuccessful American legal attempts to change the Coleman decision, the airlines were encouraged to begin legal action in January 1977, but this was also delayed while the new American President, Jimmy Carter, became established. The Port Authority continued to put off the decision for as long as possible, but a meeting between it and the airlines was arranged for 9 March. This was followed by a more detailed presentation on 1 April when a very comprehensive study of Concorde operations at Kennedy was handed over. This document, known as the 'grey book', took into account the local weather conditions over a year, to determine the likely runways to be used at Kennedy, which populated areas would be affected, and to what degree. As much of the flying as possible was to be over the sea, and here Concorde's high manoeuvrability was a great help. Because Concorde was particularly good at crosswind and tailwind take-offs, the most critical runways facing heavily populated areas could almost always be avoided. Also, as New York to London with its prevailing tailwinds was well within Concorde's range, the take-off would be lighter, requiring less power and giving a greater climb capability. It was therefore anticipated that Concorde operations would make no noticeable difference to the communities' total exposure to noise.

Having presented this evidence it was felt by both Britain and France, that if the Port would not

remove the ban, then litigation would have to provide the answer. When no response came, a court hearing was finally convened when the Port was severely criticised for delaying so long without making a decision, and also for not allowing test operations. On 11 May the ban was overturned, but the Port immediately appealed and the ban was reintroduced temporarily to allow further discussions. On 14 June the ban was upheld, but was only sustainable if it was 'fair, reasonable, and non-discriminatory'. The original court declared the ban illegal, because it was unreasonable and the second appeal was rejected. On 17 October the US Supreme Court finally declared in Concorde's favour.

Air France and British Airways promptly announced that two days later the aircraft would arrive on a proving flight and extra noise-monitoring stations were erected around the airport. The French development aircraft 201, F-WTSB, left Toulouse on 19 October bound for New York, the approach being over Jamaica Bay. Expecting a hostile welcome, it was with much surprise that the crew saw a line of hovering helicopters down either side of the approach path. The noise monitors recorded the low figure of 105.5PNdB on the approach, a level which was quite acceptable. On touch-down, the runway and the subsequent taxiways were lined with just about everyone who could obtain an airport pass, and only a few appeared hostile. Over 500 members of the press were waiting in the hangar, many from the local communities, and although their questions were searching, they were very polite.

The next day saw the first take-off, the departure procedure requiring a 25° banking turn after lift-off to keep to the edge of the bay and reduce the power over Howard Beach residential area. Shortly before Concorde's turn for take-off, the runway in use had changed, and while the observers waited, a Boeing 707 took off, followed by a Boeing 747. Both aircraft struggled a little on their turn after take-off; when Concorde followed it turned so easily and the noise was so low that the take-off seemed unexciting. The noise monitor was set to operate at a level of 105PNdB or more, and it was not even triggered off by Concorde. On landing the noise levels were again low, and better than a number of the subsonic aircraft operating at the time. Following this decisive demonstration all opposition to Concorde collapsed and the specially formed group of objectionists disbanded. Concorde had been allowed to demonstrate its capabilities, and the theoretical objections had been unfounded.

On 22 November 1977 Air France and British Airways departed from Paris and London for the inaugural passenger service to New York, the route for which the aircraft had been conceived. As on the Washington inaugural the two aircraft crossed the Atlantic in tandem, this time led by Air France, to make a joint arrival. After landing they posed together for photographs before taxying to their respective terminals. The New York Chamber of Commerce celebrated the City's entry to the supersonic age, following the 20-month delay, by holding a banquet lunch for about 1,000 guests.

Although the Washington flights had been achieving 80% load factors, these eased off and the New York route achieved similar popularity, many of the passengers being regulars. Not all the passengers were business people, because those who could afford to fly Concorde for leisure avoided the problem of jet lag.

One promising extension to the North Atlantic routes were operations by Braniff Airlines to

Below:
Air France Concorde 205 F-BVFA was the first delivery to the airline 19 December 1975. *Air France*

Bottom:
The initial Air France commercial service was from Paris to Rio de Janeiro, Brazil with Concorde 205 F-BVFA 21 January 1976. *Air France*

Top right:
British Airways Concordes being prepared for departure at London Heathrow. *BA*

Centre right:
Concorde 201 G-BOAD was painted in Singapore Airlines livery on the port side, and retained British Airways livery on the starboard side. This aircraft operated the joint service from London to Singapore.

Bottom right:
Concorde 206 G-N94AA to operate the Braniff service from Washington DC to Dallas, Fort Worth, flown by Braniff crews. *BA*

Dallas Fort Worth in Texas. The overland flights were subsonic, but linked the oil state with Europe. For these flights Braniff supplied the crews and the registrations were modified to cover the dual nationality of the crews, taking over one from the other. Regrettably, the high cost of fuel caused this route extension to be closed down in 1980. British Airways now flies three times a week to Washington, returning the next day, and two daily return flights to New York. Such modest utilisation can hardly justify the number of aircraft available and therefore both airlines find Concorde a financial burden, which from time to time, has been something they would prefer not to have. However, as a prestige airliner it is still a world beater.

Above:
Concorde 212 G-N94AE (G-BOAE) featured a dual registration for operation by British Airways crews to Washington DC and Braniff crews to Dallas. *BA*

Below:
British Airways and Air France Concordes at Dallas after their inaugural flight 12 January 1979. *BAe*

7 Concorde Operation

Concorde's primary purpose is to carry passengers significantly faster than any other form of public transport. An example of this form of high speed travel is by Air France Concorde from Paris to New York which I have been fortunate to experience personally.

Air France schedules have now been reduced to one daily flight from Paris to New York with four Concordes allocated to this service. The other three aircraft owned by Air France are held in reserve and used for spare parts. To operate the New York service there are two aircraft at each base, the morning arrival remaining overnight at each destination and returning the following day. This procedure is the standard and normally followed one. However, if a VIP, royal or political, is on the passenger list, and also

What can be achieved in 300 hours of air travel?

| | Number of Return Trips | | |
| | 1956 | 1970 | 1976 |
			Concorde
London to Sydney	1	2	4
+London to Tokyo	0	2	4
+London to New York	2.5	5	9
+London to Johannesburg	1	2	4
300 hour total	4.5	11	21

Air France Concorde 205 F-BVFA taxying out to the runway at Charles de Gaulle Airport, Paris. *Air France*

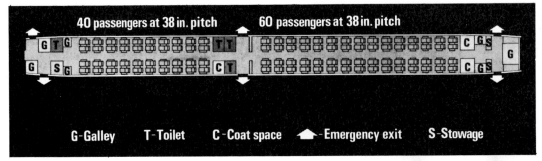

40 passengers at 38 in. pitch 60 passengers at 38 in. pitch

G-Galley T-Toilet C-Coat space ▲-Emergency exit S-Stowage

British Airways 100-seat layout. *BAe*

providing that the incoming aircraft has not experienced technical problems en route, then the same aircraft is turned around for departure without the overnight layover, as a security precaution.

There are 12 aircrews allocated to the Air France Concorde operations, consisting of 12 captains, nine first officers (second pilots) — because captains can operate as second pilots — and 12 flight engineers. The Concorde flight deck has four seats, allowing a supernumery crew member to sit behind the captain. The cabin crews consist of six pursers, 12 stewards and 18 stewardesses. The flight deck and cabin crews remain overnight in New York working an average of four to five round trips every month.

The aircrews consulted consider Concorde the 'ultimate' aircraft to fly. Due to the shorter flight times of $3\frac{1}{2}$ hours the flight deck crew obviously

become less fatigued, as compared with the seven hours flying a Boeing 747 over the same distance. Despite this reduced fatigue, Concorde operations are very much more demanding due to the high speeds which require a greater level of concentration, alertness and response to the various stages of flight. The aircrews flying Concorde are the most senior and experienced staff. The flying crews are required to report for duty two hours prior to departure and finish approximately 30 minutes after landing. Although the Air France check-lists are in French, the cockpit labelling is in English, no doubt reflecting the BAC responsibility for this section of the aircraft.

The cabin crew likewise have relatively short duty hours, but the passenger service during the transatlantic flight demands considerable energy. This service usually takes at least two hours and pushing the loaded trolleys up the aisle is very strenuous due to the high nose attitude of the aircraft. The cabin crews are also highly experienced and are especially chosen for Concorde duty. They rotate on a three-monthly basis between Concorde and subsonic jets.

Cabin cross section. *BAe*

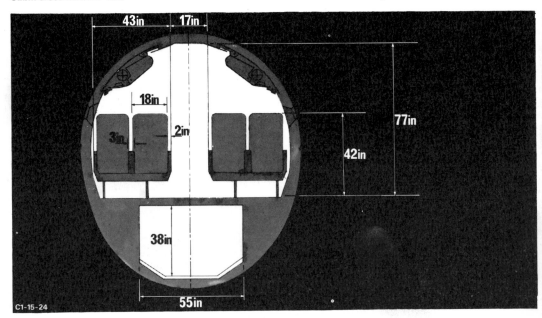

Every Concorde passenger is a VIP. At Paris, Charles de Gaulle Airport, there is a special Air France check-in desk at Terminal Two, but if the passengers are arriving in transit, they are taken directly to the Concorde lounge. In the lounge, the passengers are presented with a Concorde folder which contains the current Air France in-flight magazine, Concorde stationery, Concorde postcards, and a special certificate which can be signed by the aircrew if so desired, to commemorate the journey. The lounge itself is luxuriously furnished and whilst waiting for departure the passengers may enjoy refreshments.

Twenty minutes before the scheduled time of departure, the passengers are boarded through the low headroom entrance door which is just aft of the cockpit. There are two cabins each with four abreast seating in pairs either side of the aisle, and overhead luggage bins are provided for smaller items. The aircraft seats are pre-allocated according to passenger preference, many preferring the front cabin probably due to the lower level of aerodynamic noise. The digital Machmeter is displayed on the forward bulkhead of each cabin, and this is the only indication to the passenger of supersonic speed. The galleys are situated in the nose and tail, and the washrooms are in between the two cabins.

Compared with the more spacious wide-bodied aircraft, Concorde's cabin is relatively narrow. However, the time spent crossing the Atlantic is dramatically less, and therefore the smaller dimensions of the aircraft are perfectly adequate. The passengers' view is somewhat restricted, but this is not a criticism because there is practically nothing to see at high altitudes. The food and beverage service is of the highest quality; the meal is composed of several courses and an appropriate wine or spirit is served accordingly. Standard size bottles are used throughout, and the wines are of the very best vintage. The menus differ for the Paris to New York and the New York to Paris route and are completely replaced every few months.

During the flight, every passenger receives a Concorde cosmetic bag in either a ladies' or a men's version. Towards the end of the flight all passengers receive a gift; in my case it was a leather wallet and on the return journey the gift was a beautifully crafted pewter ashtray.

Concorde start-up and push-back is much like that of any other jet airliner, with the two inner engines started on the gate, and the outer two when the tractor is disconnected. For the taxying and take-off the nose is drooped 5° with the visor down and immediate progress is made to the runway threshold without the usual delaying queues because Concorde operates on a different timescale to the subsonic airliners.

The most noticeable feature of the take-off is the high degree of bank immediately after departure thus avoiding noise nuisance to the neighbouring populated areas. The noise monitors at the airport are normally not tripped off by Concorde and therefore departure goes unregistered. When departing from New York Kennedy Airport, for example from Runway 31 Left, Concorde turns sharply to the left after take-off before crossing

Air France Concorde 205 F-BVFA. *Air France*

Air France Concorde F-BTSD 213 being prepared for flight AF002 from New York, Kennedy Airport.

Tom Stierli

the airport boundary, and flies out over the bay. Nevertheless, there is no feeling of discomfort in this large aircraft which handles like a fighter aeroplane. After take-off the nose and visor are raised reducing aerodynamic noise in the cockpit. Visibility is still good and it is not uncommon to see other aircraft crossing in front on departure from New York. When leaving Paris, Concorde must remain subsonic until reaching the French coast, but out of New York, Mach 1 is reached much sooner after a fast and steep climb over the Atlantic.

Reheat is used for extra power on take-off and then reselected at Mach 0.95 to take the aircraft up to its cruising altitude of 59,000ft, and Mach 2.00. In the cockpit there is no sensation of breaking the sound barrier, the only indication being on the instrumentation as the shock wave moves over the sensors. There is also no sensation of switching the reheat on, the indication on the flight deck being a much increased fuel flow. The aerodynamic controls are kept in the neutral position, the climb rate being controlled by the movement of the fuel altering the position of the centre of gravity. The increase in speed is very gradual, despite reheat, between Mach 0.95 and 1.7 due to the high drag to be overcome, but the acceleration improves from 1.7 to around Mach 2.0. The normal cruise varies between Mach 1.99 and 2.02 depending on the outside air temperature. There is very little wind effect at the high altitudes flown by Concorde, the flight in

either direction over the Atlantic being of similar duration. There is however sometimes very slight clear air turbulence, but this is never as violent as at the altitudes flown by subsonic jets. A typical flight will use nearly 75,000kg of fuel, out of the 88,000kg carried. The average flight from Paris to New York will be in the air for 3hr 20min and fly in excess of Mach 1 for 2hr 40min.

Despite the high level of automation, the Air France Captain on my return flight enjoyed flying Concorde as much as possible himself. Automatic landings are made when requested by the engineering staff, or when required by poor visibility, but otherwise they may be made manually. With the nose drooped to 12° and the visor down, the view down to the runway lights is excellent. A typical landing speed for Concorde is 190mph (300km/hr).

The Air France daily Concorde flight, number AF001, leaves Paris CDG Airport at 11.00hrs and arrives at New York JFK Airport at 08.45hrs, allowing a full working day upon arrival. The return flight, number AF002, leaves New York at 13.00hrs and arrives at Paris at 22.45hrs. This rapid mode of travel largely removes any feeling of jet lag or fatigue of air travel.

Concorde passengers cannot be type-classed. They vary between one-timers who want to experience flying on the most advanced airliner in the world, businessmen who utilise the aircraft as a time saver, and vacationers who have the funds and wish to travel faster and more luxuriously. Perhaps the most demonstrative use of Concorde is by the business passengers to whom time is invaluable, who travel from Paris on the morning flight, hold a meeting in downtown New York and return on the afternoon flight.

Air France load factors are about 51% but as the economic situation improves, higher load factors could take the Concorde costs past the

break even point. Concorde operations by Air France are guaranteed throughout 1984, despite earlier rumours to the contrary, and possibly also for at least a further five years. British Airways announced an operating surplus in 1983 on its Concorde operations, while Air France had reduced its deficit to approximately £1 million annually. British Airways operates the much more popular London to New York route twice daily and the London to Washington route three times a week, giving a more profitable utilisation of its Concorde fleet and crews.

Both airlines undoubtedly gain considerable prestige from their Concorde operations, and

Above:
Air France Concorde 207 F–BVFB framed by 209 F–BVFC. *Air France*

Below:
Loading the catering on British Airways Concorde at Bahrain. *BA*

because there is adequate life in the aircraft, operations will probably continue until the end of the century, especially at the current low utilisation.

Above:
Loading and preparing Concorde G-BOAA 206 at Bahrain. *BA*

Right:
Refuelling at Bahrain. *BA*

Below:
The Air France Concorde departure lounge in Number 2 Terminal at Charles de Gaulle Airport, Paris.
Philip Birtles

Below right:
The British Airways Concorde check-in desks at London Heathrow Terminal 3. *BA*

Below:
British Airways Concorde maintenance at the London Heathrow engineering base. *BA*

Bottom:
The Rolls-Royce Olympus 593 engine removed from Concorde for maintenance. *BA*

Above:
Concorde maintenance, undercarriage functions in the hangar.

Below:
British Airways Concorde G-BOAA 206 ready to be pushed out of the engineering bases, following maintenance. *BA*

Bottom:
Air France Concorde F-BVFA on routine maintenance. *Air France*

Above left:
**Concorde rear passenger cabin
with four abreast seating for
100 passengers.**

Above:
**Passenger hand baggage on
Concorde can be stowed in
overhead bins.** *BA*

Left:
**The flight deck of Air France
Concorde F-BVFB over the
North Atlantic at Mach 1.98,
458kts.** *Philip Birtles*

Below left:
British Airways Concorde galley.
BA

8 Sales Options and Production

Concorde was designed to provide a good measure of what the consumer required — time saving. Over the optimum route London to New York, Concorde required half the time of the subsonic jet, and on long routes such as Sydney to London, instead of 24 hours, Concorde could cover the distance in just under 15 hours. Concorde could fly from London to Tokyo over the polar route in 10 hours, instead of 17 hours. Across the Pacific, Sydney to New York, would take Concorde $14\frac{1}{2}$ hours, saving eight hours on the normal subsonic times. Although not everyone wishes to pay the extra to save this time, in competitive business, such speeds can be well justified, even in the amount of interest saved on large capital sums of money.

To encourage early orders, a sales option system was devised, where the airline could pay a deposit to secure a delivery position on the production line, without being totally committed at too early a stage. Initial option takers were BOAC, Air France and Pan Am for six to eight aircraft each, all for the long range transatlantic version. By the end of 1963, five more airlines had joined the option list, consisting of Qantas for four aircraft, Continental Airlines three aircraft, Middle

Concorde Production

Aircraft	Registration	Assembled	First Flight	Delivered	Destination
001	F-WTSS	Toulouse	2/ 3/69	19/10/73	Le Bourget
002	G-BSST	Filton	9/ 4/69	4/ 3/76	Yeovilton
01	G-AXDN	Filton	17/12/71	20/08/77	Duxford
02	F-WTSA	Toulouse	10/ 1/73	20/05/74	Orly
201	F-WTSB	Toulouse	6/12/73	Retained for development	
202	G-BBDG	Filton	13/ 2/74	Retained for development	
203	F-WTSC/F-BTSC	Toulouse	31/ 1/75	6/ 1/76	Air France
204	G-BOAC	Filton	27/ 2/75	13/ 2/76	British Airways
205	F-BVFA	Toulouse	25/10/75	19/12/75	Air France
206	G-BOAA	Filton	5/11/75	14/ 1/76	British Airways
207	F-BVFB	Toulouse	6/ 3/76	8/ 4/76	Air France
208	G-BOAB	Filton	18/ 5/76	30/ 9/76	British Airways
209	F-BVFC	Toulouse	9/ 7/76	27/ 7/76	Air France
210	G-BOAD	Filton	25/ 8/76	6/12/76	British Airways
211	F-BVFD	Toulouse	10/ 2/77	26/ 3/77	Air France
212	G-BOAE	Filton	17/ 3/77	20/ 7/77	British Airways
213	F-WJAM/F-BTSD	Toulouse	26/ 6/78	18/ 9/78	Air France
214	G-BFKW/G-BOAG	Filton	21/ 4/78	6/ 2/80	British Airways
215	F-WJAN/F-BVFF	Toulouse	26/12/78	23/10/80	Air France
216	G-BFKX/G-BOAF	Filton	20/ 4/79	13/ 6/80	British Airways

East Airlines (MEA) two aircraft optioned in July, American Airlines four to six optioned in October and TWA four to six optioned in November. By May 1967, the option list had grown to a total of 16 airlines; the additions being Eastern and United Airlines six each, Air Canada four, Braniff, Japan Airlines and Lufthansa three each, Air India and Sabena two each. In the meantime, the major American airlines were also reserving delivery positions for the larger Boeing SST. In July 1972 some encouragement was given to Concorde sales, when for the first time in five years, CAAC of China placed options for three aircraft. The Shah of Iran followed with options for two Concordes in October, bringing the grand total to 79 aircraft. On the face of it, this was a very creditable order book, but the airlines were finding the fuel crisis and high interest rates crippling to their operations, especially with the introduction of the Boeing 747 on routes which could hardly fill this aircraft.

On 28 July 1972 BOAC signed a contract for

Top left:
French Concorde prototype 001 F-WTSS preserved at Le Bourget by Le Musee de l'Air was delivered 19 October 1973 following its retirement. *Philip Birtles*

Bottom left:
British Concorde prototype 002 G-BSST made its last flight to Yeovilton 4 March 1976 for preservation. *HMS Heron*

Below:
Concorde 002 G-BSST is preserved at Yeovilton by the FAA Museum on behalf of the London Science Museum. It is now under cover together with the HP115 and BAC 221 as part of an overall Concorde exhibition. *Philip Birtles*

five Concordes worth some £115million. Air France placed its order for four aircraft. A major condition of the option system was that the other airlines should confirm their orders within six months of the initial contract, and despite efforts by the manufacturers to attempt an extension of the Pan Am decision, the airline pulled out on 31 January 1973, due to the unfavourable operating economics of the aircraft. TWA followed suit. Pan Am and TWA therefore started the collapse of the sales prospects, and the whole option system was abandoned two months later with the return of the deposits. This in effect left BOAC and Air France, as the national airlines, to carry Concorde into the supersonic age on a minimum production run and without the world-wide support of a broad customer base.

Total production was eventually to reach 16 aircraft in addition to the two prototypes and two pre-production aircraft. BOAC — which became British Airways by the time of the introduction of Concorde — and Air France eventually each took delivery of seven production aircraft, although their route structure could hardly justify such a fleet size. At least one of the aircraft was rarely, if ever, used.

The first two production Concordes were retained by their manufacturers for further testing and development, leaving the remainder for airline service. The dual national assembly lines supplied their own national airlines with Concordes, and the last production aircraft was delivered from Filton to British Airways on 20 April 1979.

The prototypes and pre-production aircraft have all been preserved. The first prototype, F-WTSS, was retired to the Musée de l'Air at Le Bourget, France, after flying 812 hours and it is currently parked outside amongst the larger aircraft due to inadequate hangarage. The British prototype, G-BSST, was retired to Yeovilton on 4 March 1976 after 837 flying hours, to be in the joint care of the Science Museum and the Fleet Air Arm Museum. This aircraft was preserved initially in the open, but is now under cover as part of an overall SST display including the HP115 and BAC211 small-scale development aircraft.

The British built pre-production aircraft, 01 G-AXDN, was retired to the Imperial War Museum at Duxford on 20 August 1977 after 631 hours of test flying, and is currently pre-served in the open, but there are hopes of raising sufficient finances to provide a hangar for this and a number of the other large aircraft deteriorating outside. The French pre-production Concorde, 02 F-WTSA, was retired to public display at the Paris airport of Orly on 20 May 1974.

During 1983 there were also rumours that Concorde services might cease in 1984 due to their uneconomic operation. Even if this is so the experience that has been gained by Concorde since its inception will provide a foundation on which the next generation of SSTs can be based, possibly to allow a quieter and more economical Concorde II to enter service.

Right:
On completion of its development flying, Concorde 01 G-AXDN was retired to Duxford 20 August 1977 for preservation by the Duxford Aviation Society and Imperial War Museum. *Philip Birtles*

Right:
Concorde G-BBDG 202, retained by British Aerospace for development flying, was retired at the end of 1981 and is currently stored on the airfield at Filton. *BA*

Appendices

1 Specification

Variant: Production Version
Powerplant: Four Rolls-Royce/SNECMA Olympus 593 engines developing 38,050lb of thrust each
Accommodation: Three crew and typically 108 passengers
Fuel Capacity: 25,250gal (119,280litre)
Wing Span: 83ft 10.4in (25.56m)
Wing Area: 3,856sq ft (358.25sq m)
Length: 202ft 3.6in (61.66m)
Height: 40ft (12.19m)
Weight Empty: 174,750lb (79,265kg)
Max T/O Weight: 400,000lb (181,436kg)
Max Level Speed: 530kt over 43,0750ft (13.335m) or Mach 2.02 equivalent to 1,300mph (2,032km/hr)
Service Ceiling: 60,000ft (18.290m)
Endurance/Range: 4,313 miles (6,936km)

Concorde general arrangement. *BAe*

2 United States and Russian Competition

The United States

The major aerospace companies in the USA had been working on SST research and a range of design studies since the late 1950s. Despite the controversy of such an undertaking, the US Federal Aviation Agency (FAA) issued a Request for Proposals (RFP) on 15 August 1963 for the development of an SST. This followed a series of feasibility studies between July 1961 and June 1963. The American Government was spurred on by the competitive edge being gained by Concorde, and its intention was to produce a bigger, faster and superior SST to maintain the USA's world lead in commercial aviation. President Kennedy had already publicly backed the American SST on 5 June 1963, only two days after Pan Am had signed its purchase option for six Concordes.

The RFP called for a safe and economic SST with a mimimum cruising speed of Mach 2.2, a payload of 125 to 160 passengers, plus 2,268kg

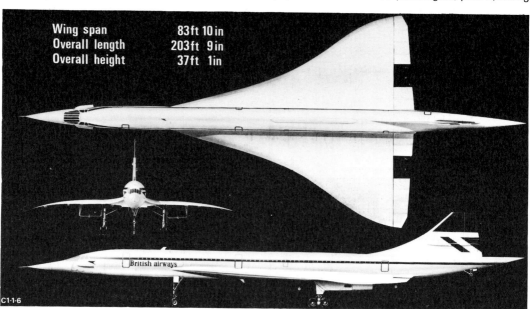

Wing span	83ft 10 in
Overall length	203ft 9 in
Overall height	37ft 1in

British airways

C1-1-6

(5,000lb) of cargo, and a range of 6,437km (4,000 miles). The development programme was envisaged in three stages, the first stage covering the initial design competition. Proposals were due by 15 January 1964 allowing a selection of the airframe and engine manufacturers following FAA and airline evaluation by 1 May 1964. The second stage was to be a more detailed competition between two airframe and engine manufacturers, if no clearly outstanding project resulted from the first stage. The third stage was the development, manufacture and testing of two pre-production aircraft. Financing of the two latter phases would be shared between the government and the manufacturer; the government providing credit assistance with production financing. It was realised that a rushed programme attempting to beat the Concorde into service would be undesirable both technically and economically. The American aircraft was hardly a direct competitor, except for airline funding, and would be complementary to the European aircraft.

The manufacturers initial proposals were disappointing. The airframes could not achieve the minimum range and payload requirements, and suffered from high direct operating costs. The engine proposals did not meet the requirements either. Boeing and Lockheed were given a further six months to improve their airframe proposals, as well as General Electric and Pratt & Whitney for the engines.

The cancellation of TSR2 by the British Government reduced the American urgency due to expected delays on Olympus engine development, and the selected US manufacturers were given a further 18 months to improve their submissions and to produce demonstration engines. Boeing teamed up with General Electric (GE) and Lockheed with Pratt & Whitney. The final evaluation of designs began in September 1966 and on the last day of the year, Boeing and GE were selected to go ahead with the prototype aircraft. This was confirmed by the US President on 29 April 1967, when 10 airlines had paid deposits on 52 delivery positions.

The resulting Boeing 2707-200 proposal featured a variable sweep wing, having been selected in favour of the slim delta-winged Lockheed design. With an overall length of 96.93m (318ft), it would be the longest aeroplane ever built. Its overall weight would be 306,180kg (675,000lb), having a typical two-class load of 292 passengers, and the cruising speed would be Mach 2.7. Power would come from four tailplane-mounted GE engines developing approximately 27,216kg (60,000lb) of thrust each. Construction would involve extensive use of stainless steel and titanium. However, this very advanced design proved to be very difficult to turn

into hardware. The swing-wing layout in particular was one of the major problems, aerodynamically as well as structurally. Despite reviews of the design with time extensions until 15 March 1968, Boeing could not produce a practical load carrying aircraft, and was instructed by the FAA to start again. The new deadline was 15 January 1969 to produce a viable design. The resulting Boeing 2707-300 was a fixed-wing delta with a conventional tail, to cruise at Mach 2.7 The take-off weight would be 340,200kg (750,000lb) and the payload 234 passengers. The design appeared close to the specification, but engine noise was expected to be a problem. The FAA recommended the construction of a prototype.

Controversy continued to grow, not helped by the arrival of a new president — Richard Nixon, who began a further investigation into the viability of the SST. In September 1969 he agreed to work continuing, but on a reduced budget. Meanwhile, opposition to the SST was mounting, especially from the environmentalists, who organised themselves into a powerful group in April 1970. With increasing political lobbying against the American SST, the final vote in the House of Representatives on 18 March 1971 deleted all funding and six days later the Senate confirmed the decision. Nearly $171million was paid out in termination costs, the total cost for no aircraft exceeding $1,035million.

The Soviet Union

The competition from the Soviet Union was significant in that the Tu144 prototype became the first SST to fly when it took off on 31 December 1968 from Zhukovky near Moscow. It reportedly exceeded Mach 1 on 5 June 1969 and Mach 2 on 26 May 1970. Its first appearance outside the Soviet Union was at the 1971 Paris Air Show. It had a similar layout to Concorde, but its four fan engines were grouped closely together. The Kuznetsov NK-144 twin-spool turbofan engines delivered a thrust of 12,973kg (28,600lb) each, increasing to 17,509kg (38,600lb) with reheat. The reheat had to be used for cruising flight as well as for take-off and transonic accelerations, making endurance too short for practical supersonic operations. The wing layout was similar to a double delta and a droop nose was fitted. The reported performance was Mach 2.35 cruise at an altitude of 20,117m (66,000ft). The passenger capacity was around 126 and the maximum take-off weight was 130,000kg (286,600lb).

At the Paris Air Show in 1973, the Tu144 exhibited was the proposed production standard with a number of major modifications, including a slight separation of the pairs of engines, a modified wing planform, and retractable canards on the fuselage high above the flight deck. The landing gear had been redesigned, and the aircraft was larger. Unfortunately, disaster struck at the show during a flight demonstration on 3 June when the aircraft went out of control and crashed on to a Paris suburb, killing all the crew and eight residents of Goussainville.

A more refined aircraft appeared at Paris in 1975, route proving flights having commenced the previous year. The first passenger flights commenced between Moscow and Alma-Ata on 1 November 1977, but are believed to have ceased in mid-1978, and nothing further has been heard of the aircraft outside the Soviet Union.

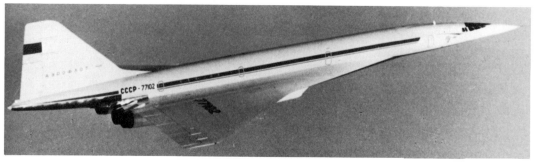

Above:
Pre-production Tu 144 CCCP 77102 with its nose and visor raised. The aircraft's lines were very similar to Concorde, but did not have the added refinement of the extended tail fuselage and the more complex double-curvature wing shape.
Courtesy Novosti Press Agency

Below:
A production Tu 144 on approach showing clearly the retractable fore-planes fitted to improve low speed control on the approach. The production Tu 144s also had more widely spaced engines than the earlier aircraft, and the undercarriage was mounted in the cowlings rather than on the wings.
Courtesy Novosti Press Agency